MY OWN
Cape Cod

Also by Gladys Taber

Country Chronicle
My Own Cookbook: From Stillmeadow and Cape Cod
Amber—A Very Personal Cat
Stillmeadow Album (Photographs by Jacques Chepard)
Especially Dogs . . . Especially at Stillmeadow
Stillmeadow Calendar
Gladys Taber's Stillmeadow Cook Book
Another Path
The Stillmeadow Road
Stillmeadow Sampler
Stillmeadow Daybook

CAPE COD

Summer is sleeping over the narrow land
As the moon lifts her casual silver sail
Over the Mill Pond, over Nauset sand.
The tides move dark and quiet to assail
The fragile yet resistant shining strand
That marks man's holding. Pale the moon's way, pale,
And I could hold the stars within my hand
Hoping against the shadows to prevail.

Summer is sleeping, and the seagulls cry
Lonely against the steeply sloping air.
Beneath the bayberry the rabbits lie
Snug in their drowsy midnight-secret lair.

Now in this hour of magic, dear love, mark
How yet God's grace makes conquest of the dark!

MY OWN
Cape Cod

by *Gladys Taber*

PARNASSUS IMPRINTS
Yarmouth Port, Mass. 02675

This edition published in 1981 by
Parnassus Imprints
Rte 6A
Yarmouth Port, Mass. 02675

Cover photograph and frontispiece
by John Schram

For Millie and Ed
Whose friendship is the mainstay of Still Cove

Spring

APRIL SONG

We rode in rain
Down a curving lane,
The boy's hair damp and flat with wet,
Lean hands on wheel so lightly set.

Carpenter's hands, I thought, grow broad of palm and thumb
And wrists grow mobile.
       "So presently we come,"
He said, "To the house I'm working on."
The car sank hard on a nothing-lawn
Pines dripped, raw wood smelled sweet
As he walked light on sneakered feet.

"I'm glad it's no development," he turned to say,
"I'd rather build a real house, one to stay."

Cape Cod is a small portion of this country. It is a peninsula poking out from Massachusetts about forty-five miles to the east, then turning north for another twenty-five. It is never more than ten miles wide anywhere. On the map, it looks like an arm, bent at the elbow, and near the joint at Orleans, which is my personal focal point, it is only three or four miles wide from the outer shore to the bayside.

Two bridges link it to the mainland, with the shining waters of the Cape Cod Canal far below them. Once you cross a bridge, a new world begins, a world of sand, marshes, bays, inlets, low cliffs and piney woods—nothing really spectacular, one might say.

Scientists tell us the Cape is young—only fifty to seventy thousand years old. Parts of New England were created around three hundred to five hundred million years ago. During the Pleistocene epoch, a sheet of ice moved from Labrador to cover all of New England. This was ten thousand feet thick at one point. As it moved south, it carried glacial deposits, including chunks of bedrock from mountains, soil, clay, boulders, and debris.

Eventually—give or take a few thousand years—the ice began to melt, and Cape Cod was born. The great boulders which rise from the sand here and there are still etched with the scratches from the glaciers' march, as if the ice itself wanted to leave a message. There are also kettleholes, deep round pools of water, where enormous ice blocks melted. Many of these have a water level above sea level and are fresh-water ponds, but there are salt ponds which connect with the sea by tidal channels. Town Cove, at Orleans, and the exquisite Salt Pond at Eastham are among the most beautiful of these. Drummer Cove at South Wellfleet is a favorite of visitors in that area.

The Cape climate has almost everything, with February being the coldest month. It is cooler in summer on the Cape than inland and warmer in winter, owing to the influence of the sea on all sides. The fierce coastal storms of winter, the Nor'easters, are balanced by the cool sea breezes in August. The heavy fogs, which are rather common, are forgotten on the blue crystal days and shining nights which follow them.

There should be around forty inches of rainfall annually, which makes gardeners happy and upsets beach visitors. But in late spring and part of summer, there are days and days like new-minted gold, when every hose in Orleans is hooked up and working overtime. On the other hand, snow is not as much of a problem as it is across the bridge, and usually melts faster.

Much of life on the Cape depends on the tides. When the tide is high, waves break on the beaches up to the line of beach grasses. In coves and inlets it is high tide an hour or so later. Six hours later the tide has receded and the beach appears again, along with mudflats.

I was reminded of this when I was at Barbara Lovely's house. She had rented a beach cottage to an inland family on a day early in the season. The tenant was on the phone in what could only be called a STATE.

"When we rented this place," he said, "the house was right on the water. When we came today there was nothing but MUD all around."

"Well," said Barbara in her soft, rich voice, "when you rent a beach house, the tides *do* go in and out. That is what tides do!"

The tide tables are printed in the newspapers and announced regularly. When the tide is low, the clam rakes and clam baskets come out. When the tide is high, swimming is better in the salt ponds and inlets and at Skaket. At low tide one may walk half a mile to get to the water at all, and it is not easy walking.

The fishing boats go out from Rock Harbor at full tide and come in again at high tide. There have been times during severe storms when the sea rose so high at Rock Harbor the fishing boats that were tied up to the pier almost floated to the parking area far above.

Scientists tell us it is the gravitational pull of the moon which causes the rise and fall of the tides, but to me this is simply another one of nature's mysteries. I can marvel at it without understanding it in the least!

The water level in the bay changes about two feet an hour and if you get too far out at low tide, it is well to watch for this change.

Spring tides average from ten to eleven feet in range and the neap tides (which come during the first and third quarters of the moon) about seven. During great storms, the tide rises so high that people have to rush to pull their boats high from the beach to the grassy slopes.

There have been any number of books written about Cape Cod, from geological studies to nature books, from classics such as *The Outermost House* by Henry Beston and *The House on Nauset Marsh* by Richardson to guidebooks and histories of the Pilgrims. There are picture books which are beautiful, and countless others. It would seem useless to write any more about the Cape!

My only reason is that my own Cape Cod is a very per-

sonal place and I long to share it. It is a place I have lived in
and loved. I have kept a journal about my experiences as a
part-time resident for a long time. Now I wish to capture the
texture of living on this narrow land as it is for me and the
people I know well.

My house is on Mill Pond—well, not on the water itself,
but a clamshell toss away at the top of the cliff. Mill Pond is a
sapphire jewel set in the circle of cliffs. These cliffs are not
like inland cliffs, fierce rock declivities, but are ancient dunes
roofed with trees and wild roses and grasses. They fold
against one another with a rhythm like folk music.

At one end of Mill Pond lies a smaller body called the
Duck Pond, as if the gods had dropped a chip from Mill
Pond herself. This is where the herons nest and the Canada
geese come to rest and diving ducks take shelter during bad
storms. We used to get in there in the canoe, paddling past
half-submerged logs and fallen trees just to fill our hearts
with quietness.

At the opposite end of Mill Pond the inlet leads to the
ocean where Nauset lies jeweled against the vastness of sky.
It is because of this inlet that both Mill Pond and Duck Pond
are salt water, although there is a place on my bank where
sweet water flows into Duck Pond and I can see the dark
color invading the blue. This is a favorite hunting ground for
seagulls, where clams are easy to take, and is the spot the herons fish. This side of it, mussels cling to the rocks, darkly
purple and rich, and deer sometimes come to drink the fresh
water.

At high tide, boats as big as Harry Hunt's *Gertrude* used
to come into Mill Pond when hurricanes were due, but the
last two years the inlet is shallower and few try it. Sailboats
and small motorboats still ride in from the outer beach.

From my windows I see the Mill Pond and the opposite
shore which used to be Mayo's Duck Farm. It was always

Top: The author's house, Still Cove. (*John Schram*)

Bottom: Still Cove seen from the shore of Mill Pond.
(*John Schram*)

white with ducks and at sunset the men came to feed them and we always tried to be home to watch. It looked as if the greening slopes were starred with a summer snowfall. Then the farm was sold, and now I see houses going up there, huge, elegant, ill-at-ease mansions. Since some of the lots cost as much as forty thousand dollars, I am sure no small Cape Cod saltbox would feel happy there!

I can also see the circle of beach around the pond, some of it shining sand and some grown over with beach grass. A Town Landing lies at the edge of the inlet and fishermen launch their boats there or come to cast. The road snaking down to it always, always, has someone walking on it, even in storms. Everyone in Tonset seems to have a compulsion to walk to the Town Landing at least once a day, with or without dogs and children. At night the police patrol car comes down, and late at night I love to see the reassuring headlights, knowing the wonderful trooper is just checking and would see any smallest glow from a discarded cigarette which might set the whole of Tonset ablaze quite easily.

There are three houses on my side of Mill Pond on a short private road which we named Blue Rock after the glacial boulder on the beach. The first is a typical Cape house, small, weathered, snug. We built it for a summer cottage before we realized we also wanted to be able to see the Cape in winter sometimes and built Still Cove, a winterized, year-round dwelling.

In between live the Barkers, who can easily be described as everyone's dream of what neighbors should be. Beyond Still Cove the road is swallowed up by piney woods, wild roses, pin oaks, nameless thickets and plenty of poison ivy. It belongs to the wild life and has not a smidgen of a path through it.

Still Cove is a low, one-story house with white cedar shingles now soft smoky gray. It has enough windows to keep my friends, the Pickniks, busy a whole day washing them come spring. A realtor would describe it as a charming Cape Codder with private beach and view, living room, large, with fireplace, kitchen, two bedrooms, bath and a half, and wing with large den-living room. I call the wing a workroom and library because every spare inch is filled with bookshelves. An antique trestle table stretches the width of the room, always covered with manuscripts, and a card table holds the overflow. Two daybeds pinch-hit as extra beds and a semi-kitchenette is tucked in one corner.

There are closets and cupboards everywhere and not nearly enough.

The only way to get to the attic is to use an extension ladder and poke up through a trapdoor in the ceiling in the hall between the living room and bath. When squirrels and mice move in, this presents a problem, and also it does not make the attic easy for storage.

The cellar is odd, too. The only way to get to it is to go outdoors and start down the steps to the beach. Halfway there is the door to the cellar. In bad weather nobody cares about going down cellar.

Opening from the cellar, on the sand terrace, is what we called the dog run. This is rather strange, for it is an Anchor-fenced area large enough for a bevy of cougars. We had the idea that on occasions when we had to be away part of a pleasant afternoon, the cockers and Irish setter could bask there, but no dog ever set paw in it except to help hang out the washing. It makes a fine drying yard with the clotheslines stretched from one side of the fence to the other!

We do not have a garage, and I often think it would be nice to have one to store cartons and firewood in and keep all the tools (it's too far to the cellar). But I am sure the car

right where it always is, nosed in toward the
window. I cannot imagine driving it into a garage
down one of those alarming metal doors.

think it over, I realize no car of mine has *ever* been
garaged except at the service station. There was a comfortable theory at the farm inland that the car would fit in the
barn, but the barn turned into a workshop, garden center and
studio, and there was only room for the lawnmower as an
extra!

While I was considering garages, I drove all around Orleans doing a little research on the subject. Generally the people who have the garage under the house, down a hazardous
pitch of driveway, do not put their cars in. The exception is
when hurricane warnings are up. The rest of the time what
goes down the driveways is rainwater, which purely loves an
easy route to the cellar. Some cellars have sump pumps on
this account.

On the other hand, houses which have garages attached to
the house—often a two-car one—are seldom what I call
beautiful. With the doors open, the effect is that of a yawning jaw growing from the end of the house. With the doors
closed, there is a resemblance to the fire station where the
trucks nest in rainy weather. The blank expanse of window-
less area is depressing.

A few residents have garages some distance from the house,
remodeled old fish houses or sheds. I always imagine how far
it seems to the house when a fifty-mile wind roars in from the
ocean or the fog is dense enough to slice with a carving knife.

As for me, I am happy to wash the dishes and look out of
the window over the sink and see my beloved Fury III looking back at me and suggesting it is time for a ride to Bridge
Road to see how the salt marsh is doing.

There is only one really noteworthy feature of the place,
which is that there is no back door. But there are two front

doors, one from the front living room and one from the hallway to the wing. Strangers who come invariably try to get in the front door farthest from where I am so that I scuttle rapidly the whole length of the house a good many times. Often packages will be delivered at the wing door and I may not see them for several days, since I am using the east door.

Aside from this, there is no place to put a trash can because who wants trash cans by a front door? Any trash collector would have to be a steeplejack to get around the two sides of the house with no front doors, and in any case the view would not be enhanced by two or three garbage containers visible from the windows! This difficulty is solved by my going to the dump every other day—always wondering if trash grows by itself or what.

Nevertheless, despite a few problems, Still Cove is exactly my idea of Heaven.

The inside of the house is not furnished in any one period, although I sometimes think it is so full of sea chests and dough chests and ancient carpenter chests that it might be called the chest period.

It also has three antique trestle or harvest tables, some small pine dropleaf tables and a very old French sewing table. My favorite is a low coffee table with drop leaves and with pegged construction. It was built by Jill, my lifetime friend, from black walnut boards. One of the aged black walnut trees at Stillmeadow crashed in a winter storm and we had the trunk cut into thick planks. The table began as a typing table for me and had high legs. When a metal typewriter table took over my machine, the table went down cellar and was used to store paint cans.

Then it came to the Cape and our friend, Ted O'Gorman, restored it, cut it down to coffee-table size and made the drop leaves from part of the top. Now, waxed and glowing, it graces the wing and is a happy link with Stillmeadow.

The chairs at Still Cove include a bevy of Hitchcock arm and straight chairs from which most of the paint has peeled (and what can I do about that?), and also several wicker Hong Kong chairs which are so comfortable and make fine scratching posts for the Abyssinian kitten. My favorite chair is a walnut straight chair which belonged to my mother.

The bedrooms are almost traditionally antique with pine headboards for the beds. The footboards had to be left out, since the rooms are not that large. The beds are really easier to make up except the bedding does sometimes slide off at the foot.

Most of the lamps were found by our dear friends Steve and Olive, who happen to be designers and decorators. They range from tin Paul Revere lanterns to cranberry glass, Bristol glass and milk glass. A few bedside lamps came direct from Snow's basement.

Actually you might say the house is chiefly furnished with books, for the only place without them is the bathroom (steam is not good for books). Except for the fireplace wall, bookshelves climb to the ceiling everywhere and books are piled on all of those chests and on the coffee table. I did save one shelf area in the wing for the stereo records.

The weather on Cape Cod is difficult to talk about in a general way, for as soon as one makes a statement about any season, the temperature changes. Nature is at her most mysterious in this narrow land. All I can say is that I have never lived any place where my furnace got so much exercise!

Friends may be sitting by the open fire warming up when suddenly the wind changes and I must turn the furnace down and open the windows. Or I am minding my own business at the typewriter with all the windows open all over the house when I suddenly notice my fingers are numb. By the time I get the windows all closed, and turn the furnace up, Amber is crouched by the bathroom heat vent which is hottest.

Now it does *not* matter what time of year it is. Everyone can talk all day in summer about the heat (which just cannot compare with inland heat in any case). In the middle of the discussion, a wind that surely must have been born on an iceberg blows in across the great vast of space and the sunbathers flee from the beaches, wrapping themselves in damp salty towels.

In the midst of winter comes a day of such promise that I have a barely controllable impulse to get the blankets on the line and start spring cleaning!

Often I start for town with the car heater on and by the time I turn off Tonset Road have the fan going. Or I decide I really should, just once, wear those sunglasses I lug around year in and year out. By the time I find them in the bottom of my shopping basket, under the magpie collection I always have, it is dark as winter twilight.

And then the sun may be dazzling on the bayside and the outer beach already drifting with fog waves until the whole world is muted to gray.

Easter traditionally belongs to parades of finery, opening flowers, egg hunts. For Christians it is a time of remembrance of the death and resurrection of Christ, a time that never loses its poignance. The story of the carpenter who died on the cross is still as heartbreaking as in our childhood when we first heard it, and the stone rolled away from the tomb still a mystery restoring hope for mankind.

This particular year, Easter came too early. I woke to see snowflakes big as butterchips swirling across a pewter Mill Pond. The junipers on the slope swayed in a melancholy rhythm. Windows rattled in the seawind. I turned the furnace up and listened apprehensively for her complaining rumble.

Amber warmed her apricot Abyssinian self by the bathroom heat vent. She emerged to inspect her breakfast tray while I fixed mine. She did not want junior beef and kitty kibbles, so she got poached fillet of flounder. I had my coffee and inevitable poached egg (I have succumbed to all the articles that say one must EAT something for breakfast). I revive my egg with a few drops of Worcestershire sauce.

The radio popped along announcing cancellation of Easter parades in Plymouth and Hyannis, and postponement of Easter-egg hunts. I doubted whether any sunrise services went on at the beaches. But I decided to try to get to Livingstons' for the Sunday *Times* and when I opened my storm door, it nearly took off into space.

People buried in winter clothing ducked in and out of the drugstore, not stopping to chat. Getting the paper was definitely not a social hour this morning. On the way home the rear window of the car frosted over and I was thankful to get back, but going from the car to the house, I bent like the handle of a coat hanger.

But as I hung my snow-frosted coat over the bathtub to drip, I reflected on the eternal quality of hope mankind has. For even in this wild storm, I felt spring was inevitable. The crocus was buried in snow, but I knew it was there. As the weather changed, the melting would be fast—it is always faster on the Cape—and the water would penetrate the sandy soil and nourish the roots of all growing things.

So I sang the closing hymn along with the Mayflower Congregational Church broadcast from Plymouth (America's Home Town). And then the ice-lace on the east picture window seemed to be diminishing already and the wind less vocal. And five diving ducks skimmed low over Mill Pond coming in to feed.

They seem to me hardier even than the seagulls, the first to come and the last to leave in bad weather. And no bird expert has ever really explained to me why they do not freeze in the icy water.

Perhaps, I thought as I watched them diving, man might yet get close to nature again and live simply in harmony with her eternal rhythms. Imagine a world without success measured by how many bodies pile up on the enemy side and how many communities are liberated by being blown to bits! Imagine an end to exploding nuclear devices in Nevada spreading poison above ground to kill all life within miles and miles. How casual we were about six thousand sheep being slaughtered out west by a small mistake in controlling poison!

Imagine an end to hunger and a real attempt to give education to all children!

At Eastertime, no matter what the weather, we can pray for new goals for world leaders to pursue. The very act of praying is an affirmation of hope, I believe, whether we pray to a personal God or an infinite unity of some kind. And all the prayers that have risen on this storm-beaten Easter may provide an inner strength.

I looked out through the snow curtain at the dark Mill Pond and waved to the small ducks who could not possibly see me.

"Good fishing," I called to them, "and some shelter for the night."

I watched the diving ducks on Mill Pond yesterday. They skim so fast over the blue-green salt water that I cannot count them. They skitter, wings fluttering, but feet in the pond. It is a method of locomotion man has not mastered.

At some mysterious signal, they begin to dive, and simply vanish. A school of small fish or minnows must be visible then in the unpolluted depths. They stay down longer than I can hold my breath, although I try. Gasping and red-faced, I hear my heart pumping in my ears. I give up. Then the ducks emerge like popping corn, obviously not even breathless because they begin skimming again at once.

I do not see them swallow, and imagine they gulp their prey under the surface, but why don't they choke eating underwater?

The hawk planed in at dusk last night. He was coasting on air currents over the wooded shore. Not a bird was stirring; for him the next meal was problematical. I felt his hunger and thought of his lonely flight and wished I could set out something he would eat. I do not make moral judgments on any living creature except man and I try not to do that any more than necessary. So I wished him well.

The hawk is a born predator, but so, in a way, are all creatures. The hawk does not kill his own kind. The great swooping angles of his flight give one an ominous feeling but also a sense of unleashed power we all long for at times. Could we arrow down on a target with such speed and such beauty of flight?

I find it too easy to identify with the tiny song sparrow crouching on her nest and also with the coasting hungry hawk as the shadow of the hawk wings falls on the shingle where the tide is going out. The sand is the color of pirate's gold and receives the wing shadow plainly.

When I drive down Tonset Road to town, the stillness of early spring is there. The sunlit lawns are empty except of crocus clusters. The saltbox houses seem asleep. I seldom see anyone or hear a car motor but the summer people are not yet here.

Emperor tulips will soon bloom in the prettiest garden

along with jonquils and daffodils. The Emperor, I am told, is
the only tulip easy to manage on the Cape because rabbits do
not like the taste, and the overpopulation of rabbits destroys
anything else considered edible, including all of my special
roses.

Right now even the rabbits are invisible.

The Cape sunlight has a clarity I have never seen anywhere
else. Perhaps the vast expanse of ocean on all sides and the
countless small salt ponds may reflect extra light which
woods and fields inland swallow up. It is not a hard diamond-
like light but reminds me of melted crystal (if that could be).
I spend a great deal of time looking at this sunlight and trying
to capture it in words.

On Tonset Road now, it etches charcoal shadows on every
shingle on the house fronts and under the shutter slats. Most
of the houses are white or natural weathered cedar, but the
trim and shutters express the owner's favorite color—
daffodil yellow, lime green, black, cherry, blue—and
front doors are often painted to match the trim. The sunlight
now in early spring gives a polished look to the colors, inten-
sifying them, making them glow.

I drive slowly, feeling lost in a dream. I am reminded of
Lyonnesse that sank beneath the aquamarine sea in legendary
times and could sometimes be seen glimmering in the depths.
Could Tonset Road and I sink quietly down into Town
Cove?

Across from the old cemetery, I look at Sea Call Farm but
Miss Fiske is not out in her garden as she usually is. Nights
are too cold, the ground is not plowed. Miss Fiske raises flowers to sell and has a big garden which slopes from the house
to the road and is burnished with color all summer long. She
cuts bouquets and sets them in the cool dark of a shed, in
green and white and blue mixing bowls. Few professional
flower arrangers could match her arrangements. I have writ-

ten two books on flower arranging, but when I buy bouquets from Miss Fiske I carry them with an effort not to disturb one single posy.

In back of the old shed—or barn—sits her car, covered with sheets of plastic, for she no longer drives. It is sad to see it there, shadowy and silent. However, there is plenty of noise from her bevy of attack dogs who stay in a nearby run during the day. They protect her, companion her, sleep and eat with her, but go to the run to save the lives of visitors who only want bouquets!

Last summer one of the oldest dogs fell ill and I stopped in often to discuss symptoms. Kim Schneider, our beloved veterinarian, did all he could but could not save the dog. When he died in the hospital, the Orleans police brought the body back in a squad car so Miss Fiske could bury him in her own yard and plant flowers on his grave.

In my particular Cape town, the police do not resemble those we read about in Chicago. Chet Landers, the chief of police, is a big, craggy-faced man with a quiet voice and a smile, warm and reassuring. He and the police force are always available, and the time I called them when a crowd of drunken youngsters invaded my beach, the squad car was there in twenty minutes. It takes me twenty-five to get to town over the same route.

It is, I think, an extra dividend when you can be in an area and feel that if anything is wrong, a phone call brings help. When Amber, my Abyssinian kitten, slipped out of the door and skimmed toward the beach my first thought was, "I'll call Chet." But fortunately a tall, lanky, polished officer did not have to plunge down the steep bank of poison ivy, for my young neighbor, Holly Morrison, was walking her combination-type of puppy below on the beach and I shouted at her to RUN to the steps and start up with Cricket.

It is probably a two-hundred-foot drop from my yard to

the beach and I could not possibly get down the steps as fast as an Abyssinian. But Holly and Cricket came panting up from below so fast that Amber decided she liked home better than the wide open spaces.

The second time I looked for the police was when I saw an Irish setter limping through traffic on Main Street. I tried to get through the stream of cars to reach her but the summer bumper-to-bumper traffic was on. When I finally got to the traffic stop signs there was an officer there and I flew over, letting drivers honk away behind me.

When I told him, he said, "I'll get a squad car to circle around and try to pick her up." Then he added the most comforting words one can hear, "I'll take care of it."

The main subject of conversation in town is when the summer people will be coming. When I graduated from being classified as a summer person (I do not leave until November), I felt as if I had won the Medal of Honor. We all agree the season begins earlier and earlier. Even now out-of-state cars are parked at the market and at Snow's hardware, stationery, appliance and everything-else store. People have stolen a weekend to come and "open the cottage."

I have thought about the problem of summer people for a long, long time. And I state without reservation that courteous, thoughtful, sensible visitors always find a welcome. But those who come and strew garbage along the roads, drop small kittens as they leave, pile up beer cans on the beautiful beaches, walk barefoot in the stores and drive fifty miles an hour on the narrow streets build up an image of invasion Cape Codders do not like.

The typical Cape remark is, "You must meet the Careys. Of course they are summer people but they are the nicest couple—and someday they want to cross the bridge for good."

As with most things in this confused world, man shapes his own image.

The wind blows. At night it has a two-toned sound like part of a chord on an electric guitar. The first time I heard it, I opened the door to see who was out in the dark in my yard. Inland wind does not make the same sound, but when the seawind blows in from Nauset, the throbbing of the surf comes with it.

The sound of the surf is really the theme song of the Cape, for you hear it whether you are on Monument Road or Chickadee Lane or Barley Neck or Defiance Lane. Cape Codders need this reassurance that the sea is her own, still unconquered by man. Standing around in the small country store on an early April day, someone says, "Frost again last night."

"Remember the May it snowed?"

"Did you hear the surf last night? Woke both of us out of a sound sleep. Big one out at sea, surely."

We have surf on Mill Pond too, making soft thunder. Mill Pond is, as I have said, really an extension of the ocean by way of an inlet that comes from the Nauset side of the Cape. As time goes on, the inlet is gradually silting in but small boats still make it in at high tide.

Still Cove, my house, faces east, so I can watch sunrise over Nauset, visible in the distance, but I am more likely to see the sunset from my studio windows on the other side of the house. There is the apricot glow and the tips of the pines black-green. Then I know it is time to drive across town to Rock Harbor where the sun drops into the emerald sea.

Wednesday the Full Pink Moon shone over Mill Pond around one o'clock. The moon moves from the Nauset side to the Rock Harbor side, crossing Mill Pond in her journey. On clear nights the moonpath in the water is wide enough to walk on, polished gold. Ripples all over the surface are brushed with peach color.

The sound of the peepers is loud in the night. Beyond Still Cove the land slopes down to Duck Pond and is heavily wooded with pine, some pear and wild apple trees and some red maple. The peepers are down there along with frogs and other wild creatures and Canada geese getting ready to move.

This land was all one big farm in the beginning when the Cape still had occupations other than fishing, cranberries and tourists. If you push through the thickets you find old stone fences marking field lines. I am sure the pear and wild apple trees are leftovers from that day, a special heritage. One pear stands in the middle of a bevy of pines, a pin oak and a tangle of bayberry bushes. I can see this pear from the kitchen window when it blooms. The long slender branches reach like tapers to the sky, glowing with delicate blossoms. This is an early-blooming tree but right now is only faintly blurred with budding.

The April Mill Pond has three or four small boats riding out the winds. Summer pleasure craft are blessedly absent. Two or three men in the neighborhood climb down the steep hill to the beach, then wade out in high boots and haul the boats inshore so they can bail them out and up anchor and go fishing. They hunch against the bitter wind. The burning orange of those insulated jackets is probably the most hideous color in the world but is a safeguard, for an observer can see that orange as far as an eye can see anything.

The clammers wear them also. A neighbor clams on my beach and came up the steps dripping today, with a bucket of sweet clams for my supper. As I scrub them and wash them with cold water, I begin to compose a Sonnet for Steamers. But by the time they are in the clam kettle with barely enough water to cover, and the butter is melting in the copper ramekin and the onion-pattern soup bowl is on the table, I forget about verse.

The broth may be strained into a mug. The clams should be dipped in butter, in broth, and eaten in happy silence. But if friends are with you, there is always the argument as to whether you dip first in the broth (to clear any bit of sand) or first in the butter so a little butter drips in the broth and enriches it. I settle the problem by alternating!

As to how many clams per person my cherished friend Slim Lovely can eat, he admits, several dozen. He is thin as a willow branch and tall, and most women who see him long to make apple pies for him. But a man who can eat four dozen clams does very well!

My nearest neighbor, Pret, has his lobster pots out this week. They stay out of the water all winter, then he paints the buoys, soaks the pots in the salt water, rows out with them, fills them with bait and lowers them in the cold Mill Pond. They are awkward and heavy and it is a tiring, messy job. Pret is not a commercial lobsterman but he has a private, family license for eight—or maybe ten—pots. I always watch him when he rows out to check them late in the day, and when he heaves especially hard, I know he has a lobster for Kay to cook for supper.

The seagulls swoop over when anyone is on the water. They ride the air currents like kites. When the tide is out, they strut along the shingle or wet sand and hunt for clams. When they find a clam, they fight over it, then the winner rises high in the air and drops it on the rocky landing to break the shell. He plummets on it the minute it hits the stones.

When it comes to lobstering, Harry Hunt is a legend in his own time. He is said to go out in his sturdy fishing boat as much as a hundred miles or more off shore. He knows all there is to know about lobsters and the ocean and the weather.

Young clammer after soft shells. (*John Schram*)

Cape weather seldom coincides with the weather reports. I often wonder why the Boston forecasters, at least, never lift up a telephone and call Hyannis and ask if it is raining or blowing. But they don't, obviously, for Don Kent and the other broadcasters will say, "This is a clear, warm day." It will be pouring and a bitter gale blowing right at the minute.

But Harry Hunt never makes mistakes. I pay no attention whatever to the forecasters as to hurricanes or Nor'easters. But if I get up in the morning and see Harry Hunt's boat anchored in Mill Pond under my windows, I call up a few friends and announce the hurricane is on the way, Harry Hunt says so.

Harry's lobster boat is named *Gertrude*. There have been several *Gertrude*s, for the name never changes even when a new boat is launched. Somehow I like a boat named *Gertrude* better than *Sea Rover* or *Explorer* or *Sinbad* or *Dolphin*.

Mrs. Hunt (Gertrude) is an Eskimo but does not resemble the pictures of the traditional fur-suited person lost in a parka. She is a handsome, small, stocky woman with a better carriage than most women I have known. Her shiny dark eyes crinkle with humor and her smile is quick. Her skin is the color Cape visitors labor all summer to get and then lose inland.

I met her at the post office last week and after a small chat she started on out. I opened my box and a whole cascade of mail went to the floor. Before I could even lean over, Gertrude was back inside, scooping up the mail with a swallow-flight swiftness. I often do drop mail when the box is full and I bend painfully to gather it up as people come and go, often almost stepping on my mail.

It won't surprise anyone to know I feel warmly toward Mrs. Harry Hunt!

The lobster industry has a dubious future, if any. Illegal trapping of too young females, dragging up under-size males, and so on have threatened the whole existence of the lobster. It takes, I am told, 7½ years for a lobster to be at its peak of development, since it is one of the most slowly growing of creatures. It is strange that when man enjoys something, he invariably destroys it.

There was a time when Wellfleet oysters were shipped to Boston. They were bigger and sweeter than any others and boats plied back and forth simply loaded with them. Eventually the beds were stripped and the few weaklings left succumbed to some kind of borer.

Now the father of one of my dearest friends (Jimmy De-Lory), who was a long time oysterman, has his private bed near his home in Wellfleet. Pappy DeLory brings a pail of oysters to Orleans now and then, and I am fortunate enough to go over to Jimmy and Eileen's and eat the most delectable fare on this planet. Pappy can take a look at an opened oyster and tell you how old it is and what sex. All I know is how plump and shiny and savory it is.

Sometimes in early spring I try to imagine what the Cape was like in the Pleistocene epoch when the ice sheets produced this peninsula. But who am I to question twenty thousand years more or less when I cannot remember when I left the laundry last at Acme?

Time, to me, is now. My mind is too finite to envision either billions of dollars spent on missiles which may blow up the planet or billions of years during which some other planet may evolve. Time is five o'clock this morning when I saw a last-quarter moon moving over Duck Pond and a peach-colored glow over Nauset as the sun contemplated another journey to establish another day for Cape Cod.

I happen to think boulders are beautiful, possibly because my father was a geologist and our house was always full of rock with various striations proving something about glacial till. On my beach at Mill Pond are granite rocks, some pink, some gray. There are several that I spend much time looking at. They are two or three feet high and shaped exactly like pyramids. The tips make nice seagull-perching spots. Rising from the shell-and-sand beach, they have a magic appearance. My father would know just how the ice sheet made them, and from whence they came.

I spend my time wondering what the Egyptians saw that was this shape they wanted to copy for the pyramids they built.

Below the house there is Blue Rock, which named this short private road with three houses on it. It is a giant boulder, a gray-blue. When we first came here for a week, we met old Cap'n Dan, who was ninety and lived in a small clapboard house down the road.

"Oh yes," he said. "You are the girls staying over by Blue Rock." So we knew its name.

Nature's process is at work, as always, for a fault line developed in the midst of the massive rock mass some time ago and the rock is slowly diminishing year by year. It is now, after fifteen years, low enough for the grandchildren, ten and eight, to clamber to the top and pretend it is a pirate ship. Eventually it will split along that fault line and become two boulders. No doubt Papa would have estimated how many hundreds or thousands of years it will be before Blue Rock is a pebble stretch of beach and how many before it is sand.

Nothing is static about nature. The eastern shore of the Cape has been cut back two or three miles at a rate of two or three feet a year, according to the Geodetic Survey during the nineteenth century.

Along Nauset beach, when we first came, a line of telephone poles wandered off to the left, going nowhere. Once, they told us, there were cottages there, long since vanished as the sea moved in.

U. S. Coast Guard Station, Eastham. (*John Schram*)

At the Eastham Coast Guard beach, the Outermost House made famous by Henry Beston has been moved farther inland as the hungry tides eroded the beach. All attempts to establish pilings or breakwaters have failed. The sea is changing Cape Cod. One scientist hazards a guess that in thirty-five hundred years we shall lose two miles of coastline. Of course one can reflect that unless governments change radically, the Cape will be blown up before that time.

The bay side is more protected, and Skaket and Rock Harbor have changed little since I first saw them. The hazard for them is already man, for every little while someone decides to pave whole sections of marsh, digging out the beautiful beach grass and making parking lots where the shining sands make magic for children and weary adults and birds. So far, conservationists have saved the beaches as well as some of the salt marshes but not enough of them.

When the early settlers came, the Cape was heavily forested and teeming with wildlife and fish. Now the great forests are gone and most of the woodlands are low in growth. Some visitors from inland states where there are still true forests complain because they say the Cape is barren.

Some residents go annually to Vermont, Maine and New Hampshire to see the autumn coloring. Newspapers publish bulletins announcing just when to go! However, the true Cape addict finds the Cape dazzling in fall. (I shall explain this later.)

There were enormous elms in Orleans once, as in most of New England, but every year more of the beautiful canopied trunks go down as the Dutch elm disease takes its fatal toll. On my way down East Main, great raw stumps bleed in the sun and I try to look the other way and enjoy as a compensation the budding tulip trees and green-golden fountains of the willows at the corner of Tonset and Main.

The trees that grow in my small woods make me wish I

had taken less French in college and more botany. There are
varieties of pine that I can't identify, from the close-set taper-
ing fir to the scraggly long-needled kind with Christmas-can-
dle tips. There is a soft kind with a lacy look. There are also
the wild fruit trees I mentioned, and a few half-choked pin
oaks (I have none of these on the thirty-eight acres in Connecticut).

Scrub oak fills any free space, and then there are the bayberry bushes. From the west window I see a pinky glow
which is a red maple just coming into leaf. I don't know what
it is doing there since I always thought this tree—we call
them swamp maples—likes to grow at the edges of swamps
or in damp, boggy places.

This woodland is so thickly grown that nobody could get
through it without an axe. So what there is in the middle of
it, I cannot guess and since I am leaving this as my gift to nature, I shall never know.

The land slopes steeply—it really pitches; slope is too
gentle a word—and the Mill Pond sends her tides across
the narrow sand and beach grass below. But the woods grow
right down to the line of the beach, which means this growth
withstands the Nor'easters, the hurricanes, the wintry winds
and the blown salt from Mill Pond when storms scoop the
water up.

My windows, on top of the bluff, are crusted with salt
after a bad storm. The television antenna is pitted with it.
Paint peels from the window casings facing the water as if it
had been scraped off. Windowsills rot.

So how, I wonder, do the trees and shrubs thrive?

I also wonder whether the fact they grow in such an im-
penetrable mass is a form of protection against the bitter sea
winds in winter. The open woods inland at Stillmeadow offer
no resistance to a ten- and eight-year-old, but when the children are on Cape Cod, they gravitate to the beach.

Wildlife has problems. One April day I sat at my desk and looked out at the changing color in the woods and suddenly a pair of young deer came leaping out and began to play games on the plate-sized lawn. They were the symbol of all that is free and full of grace, and I felt quick tears salting my eyes just as when I saw the delicate head of Aphrodite in the Boston Museum.

I sat very still but when they leaped nearer the window they saw me and both stood, beautiful, wary eyes on me. The window was open enough so that when I called to them, they heard me.

What do you say to two young deer? I said, "Oh, you are lovely as a dream." The tone of my voice was all that mattered. They believed me! They flickered the small cottony blobs that are not tails, stooped to nibble some sweet clover and then vanished in the woods again.

Of course I realized if I had made friends with them it would have caused their death, since we are a nation of killers. Better for them to distrust all two-legged creatures than come near a man with a gun.

The Cape being a sea-girt land, fog is common here. As I write, a dense wall shuts off the view of the ocean and the opposite shore of Mill Pond is dipped in gray veiling. The sky is visible but is lead-colored. There is enough wind to mark the grayness of Mill Pond with riffles of green.

The only sign of life is a pair of seagulls rocking on the water. No bird flies. No boat moves. No clammers on the beach. Perhaps there is no one left on earth but me and two seagulls!

I mention this because it is the special feature of a Cape fog. It gives a sense of isolation. It hides familiar landmarks and muffles sounds. Sometimes at night I have tried to drive in it and been unable to see either side of the road. Fog and

fire are the only two things I am afraid of—odd they both
begin with *F!*

But there is a beauty about fog, especially if you are tucked
up in a warm, dry house looking out. We have no words in
what seems a limited language as far as color is concerned, to
describe the variations in the grays, and gray is a silent quiet
color (a far cry from the shouting reds and oranges).

Fog has a penetrating damp, more potent than a rainfall.
For this reason even in a drought the foliage, gardens and
lawns tend to survive. The fog nourishes them. It does other
things, too. Five minutes after a trip to the beauty parlor my
hair is flat and limp on a day of fog and the inside of the car
seems like a cellar with a leak somewhere.

My Abyssinian kitten, Amber, is affected. She sits on the
windowsill staring out, her eyes onyx (in the sun when the
pupils narrow they are topaz). No birds are hopping around
the birdbath. Amber knows she will not go out in this. She
finally decides sensibly to take a nap and folds herself up neat
as a stamped envelope.

I have known one or two people in my life who claim that
weather does not affect them. I do not believe them. I may
react too intensely but I think atmospheric conditions have
an impact. I notice I move more slowly on a day of heavy
fog and have a tendency to stop in the middle of dishwashing
or dusting and stand just looking out. My heartbeat seems
slower, too. If the out-of-doors darkens around noon to a
twilight hue, I begin to think it would be nice to tuck myself
up beside Amber and take a nap, and as a non-napper this is a
staggering innovation!

Sometimes the fog drifts away, going in waves and finally
being only a charcoal-tinted bank over the sea. Sometimes a
storm moves in with gale winds and flooding rain and the
storm may be going full tilt while the fog has not yet con-
ceded the field. I am happier when the fog ribbons off and

sun streaks appear and, especially now, the golds and violets and pinks of spring flowers are reborn.

Cape Codders are intimate with weather and they rarely complain even when there are days of fog and rain. "Can always use more rain," one man said to me at the post office.

"Got to expect this. And rain doesn't have to be shoveled. Better rain than snow."

"Makes you think about those poor people in California. Guess they better come to the Cape."

"It'll dry up come August."

One April holiday I had never known is celebrated in Massachusetts with parades, costumes and closed stores. This is, April 19, Paul Revere's Day, now called Patriots' Day officially but Paul Revere's Day by my friends in Orleans. In the Almanac it is listed as Patriots' Day.

This year we had two of them, owing to the new rule about holidays being observed on Monday. The Bostonians and Cape Codders, and probably much of Massachusetts, had Paul Revere's Day as always. The spirit of independence has not vanished. On Monday, part of the business places in Orleans were closed. The post office was open, since the holiday is not a federal one.

Everyone was thoroughly confused and wandered around trying locked doors on Main Street.

Toward the end of April, the boats at Rock Harbor begin to come back to their stations by the jetty—or whatever they call it. Each fishing boat has her own stand with her name on a post in the pilings. Several are now being painted across the waterway on the sand. One is propped up on timbers on this side and a fresh coat of shocking pink was on when Margaret Stanger and I went to watch the sun set in the bay the other night.

Seal resting on light buoy off Rock Harbor. (*John Schram*)

Out of the sea, these rugged fishing boats have a defenseless look, strangely apologetic. Then when they slide into the water, they rock so gracefully in the ripples—the ugly ducklings into swans all over again.

Any time of year there are cars parked at Rock Harbor with people sitting quietly watching the bay and sunset or the boats coming in or the boats going out. Margaret remarked that they are quiet people, just sitting and looking.

"We are all touching something basic," I said, "but I couldn't analyze it."

The old lightship is still there, silhouetted against an opal sky. She was once a Liberty ship, they say. Now she is the target for training bombers. The bombs are bags filled with flour, I am told, but I can hear them way across the Cape when they have been dropped.

My dear friend Bobby Gibson rowed out once and reported the hull was full of holes and the ship rested on a sandbar which kept her from sinking. The iron sheathing was red with rust. Bobby was then around thirteen.

But the old lightship is still there and gives a kind of reassurance to everyone who goes to watch the sunset.

April has really all the kinds of weather there are, from bitter gales to heavy fog, from dazzling days to thunderstorms. When we built our Cape house, I was asking the builder about the lightning rods.

"Oh, we never have them," he said, with the usual Cape Cod firmness. You never argue with it.

I began driving around all the enchanting back roads inspecting the lovely, lovely saltbox houses, and I could not see any lightning rods anywhere. Now this is surprising, for Stillmeadow, in Connecticut, even has the giant sugar maples cabled with copper to protect against lightning. I wonder whether the ocean may act as a safeguard.

In any case, thunderstorms do come this time of year and

lightning seems to explode from the black heart of the thunder. Just once it was so near I felt I should phone the police.
The telephone crackled and popped and I held the receiver at
arm's length with the idea that then I would not get struck.

What that bolt did was a strange trick. It blew all of the
light bulbs at the Lovelys' on Champlain Road, about two
and a half blocks from my house. But it did *not* set fire to
anything in the big two-story house, it simply exploded the
light bulbs.

After a thunderstorm, the air glitters and the earth has a
polished look. The sand on the beach is honey-color and a
faint misty green appears in my lawn. Well, I call it a lawn
but it should be named a weed patch.

Lawn grass is not indigenous to the Cape. The sandy, grav-
elly, rocky or swampy soil encourages many growing things
—one of which I love most, the pinky wild beach grass that
grows on my farther lot near the water. But people who
want green lawns work for them feverishly.

Now I am once more amazed at man's persistence, for
some of my neighbors knock themselves out making a lawn
like a golf green. My next-door neighbor Pret, whom I
greatly love and admire, theoretically came to the Cape to retire. I doubt whether he has ever worked harder in his life,
from sunrise to dark. The area surrounding his house was
plaintain, briars, some milkweed and plenty of a curious flat
emerald weed that grows anywhere.

Every time I drive to the post office, Pret is on his hands
and knees working on the lawn or racing the lawnmower
motor as he mows it again, or spreading fertilizer or watering
it. I have known him to water it almost before it stopped
raining!

It is a magnificent lawn and anyone who drives past it and
comes to my shaggy, untrimmed, unfed yard has quite a
shock. Mine gets mowed when Bob Chandler has a few hours

off from the post office, which is seldom. It never gets ferti-
lized, for I wasn't sure what effect fertilizer would have on
the paws of a racing Irish or a dainty Abyssinian.

The second spectacular lawn in our neighborhood belongs
to Orin Tovrov (who wrote "Ma Perkins" and "The Doctors" among other scripts). Orin has a man working on his
acreage daily. Beyond that, a retired executive of a big company lives in a charming old saltbox where he grew up. He
has a buried watering system for his lawn and a special variety of grass which sometimes almost has a blue tinge, like col-
or-television faces. It always surprises me to drive past this
house and see fountains of water suddenly erupt from the
lawn.

I miss the cranberry bog that was once there, but the
owner reported that he had worked too hard in that bog,
when he was a boy, and wanted to forget it. He built a huge
tennis court over it. I suppose this is progress.

Those of us who lack the energy to nurse our lawns let
them battle for survival. In spring and summer and autumn
there is always such a wonder of flowering on the Cape, we
do not notice the thin dandelion-studded stretches.

My neighbor Jim Gibson went fishing the other night and
came home with striped bass and flounder. Cape people are
sharers, so Jim hailed me as I went by and told me to stay
right there. Then he brought out an insulated bag filled with
filleted bass and creamy pink flounder.

When I came home, Amber met me and followed me to
the kitchen, indicating plainly that fish is her favorite food.
How she smelled it through three thicknesses of wrappings
is odd, but her sense of smell is phenomenal, just as remarkable as her eyesight.

I promised her a fillet of flounder simmered in butter for
her breakfast. Mine will be for supper with a dash of lemon

juice and seasoned salt and seasoned pepper. Flounder is my
favorite of the native fish—I call them flat fish, which is
their shape. They lie on one side near the bottom of the
water, and one side is darker than the other in consequence.
They look as if they had been ironed. We used to fish for
them from our canoe when we first came to the Cape for
brief holidays, and I was known around this area as the flounder queen of Mill Pond because I usually caught two at once.

I don't like killing, so I was in constant conflict then, since
I can hardly step on a wasp that has sneaked into the living
room and crawls around the rug. Wasps fly wildly when
they are caught in an automobile and pursue an erratic,
dizzying course, but early in spring they crawl in bathtubs
and sidle along kitchen floors. I know wasps must be killed,
at least in my household, for half the family is allergic to
them. But there is always that moment of doubt.

With flounder, I shut my eyes when I pulled them in. But I
had felt the excitement of the tug on the line nevertheless and
would ultimately enjoy the delicate tenderness of the best fish
there is! Which shows how inconsistent a woman can be—
and some men are, too.

There is not much plowing on the Cape except to bulldoze
for new developments. The last two farms I know of in this
area have been sold for building lots. It is a pity, for the Cape
soil suits certain crops as few regions do. In former times,
Eastham was famous for her asparagus and even now I see a
few stalks growing wild, and wish a few people would raise
just small crops of asparagus.

That available in the grocery stores is worn out from a
long journey, is pale and limp and stringy. Amber will eat the
tips, but only because this is her favorite vegetable.

Strawberries grow plump and sweet on the Cape and once
were raised extensively. Potatoes like the sandy, light soil

also—and how hard it is to get a really good potato nowadays! We raised our own in Connecticut in the rocky soil
and always had a supper to celebrate the first digging. Jill
brought in a basket of pearly nuggets which were cooked at
once in a small amount of water with a dab of butter and
some seasoned salt in it.

We served them in soup bowls with more butter, paprika,
salt and pepper. Sometimes we had a green salad, sometimes
not. We kept the coffee hot and served fresh fruit for dessert.
The flavor of a newly dug very young potato does not resemble any other in the world as far as I know. I could never
describe it except to say it means sunset over the wooded hill,
the scent of applewood fire burning low in the fireplace and
an occasional bird note from some recalcitrant soul who feels
like staying up later than the rest.

I believe man needs to be close to the land and food should
not be synthetic, and I should like to see a part of the Cape
devoted to fruits and vegetables once more.

The Cape still has the cranberry bogs and cranberry products are a main industry. Most of the crops go across the
bridge to a processing plant where all kinds of juice and jel-
lies are made ready for the market. On-Cape a few residents
make cranberry relish and sell it in the front yard. They also
do beach plum jelly—which I will talk of later on.

The cranberry juice is the color of the black cherries I remember from my childhood, and it seems to glow when the
light strikes it. It has naturally a tart crisp taste and no refrigerator is well-furnished without it.

My patch of wild cranberry is small and only covers the
slope leading to the first landing on the way to the beach. It
was planted a long time ago by Jill when we took our first
two weeks a season on the Cape while her children and mine
were at school or camp.

Now it is full of weeds and has suffered from freezes, ex-

cept where it was *not* planted at all. It crept out onto the
sandy terrace and *there* grows beautifully. Nothing will en-
courage it where it *should* be.

There are slopes around Eastham where it makes a carpet.
They call it hog berry because it does not produce edible
berries as it does in the bogs. It does not transplant any better
than a true New Englander transplants. It has fine hairlike
roots in the sand and the slightest stirring of the sand destroys
them. Nevertheless, Jill managed to make a good bed for the
first few years.

This meant we could sit in beach chairs on the scraggly
lawn and watch the cranberry slope closely. The flowers are
pale pink and so fairylike you do not notice them as you
drive by a bog. They give me the same sense of wonder the
arbutus in the northern Wisconsin woods used to bring me.

They are in bloom now—on the piece that grows on the
terrace. The leaves are glossy green, thick as a mat.

In the commercial bogs the air will soon fill with the mysterious sound of bees who harvest their own honey. Later the
green berries hang on the delicate stalks and by September
the whole expanse of the bogs glows garnet.

If I drive down the inland roads, especially on Route 39
where I know the bogs are not replaced by motels as yet, I
like to sit and drench my always-hungry color appetite in
the flat spread of nature's color extravagance. The bogs are
peat or muck and have the ironed flatness of a real swamp
area. Of course there is sand in them too, for sand is the
Cape's signature. The cranberries carpet them with splendor.

Cranberries are harvested by tined scoops, which have been
traditional time out of mind. So far not too many mechanical
monsters sweep the bogs. As of now, men still harvest some
of the crop, moving right and left with the wooden scoops.
Most of them are Portuguese with skins the color of ripe but-
ternuts and lean, mobile bodies. Some are Bravas, half-Portu-

guese and half-Negro from Cape Verde. I admit to a strong affection for both and in the villages they live in, I never drive by without stopping to visit with anyone I see near the road.

I always feel a faint apologetic sense when I stop to talk with a road man. The easy warmth, the willingness to move four road machines so I can get by, the graceful wave of a large square hand and the goodbye leave me humble.

Back to the cranberry bogs. They can be flooded when danger of freezing comes; the water protects the plants. At that time they look as if they were wading in a special sea. They also invariably have birdhouses perched on poles. Martins are the best protection man can have, although he seldom realizes it. My dear friend Hal Borland knows how many insects and pests one bird eats in a season, but I am not good at figures so it is better to consult him. Nobody would believe me but anyone will believe him.

When the first frost comes, the cranberry bogs begin to glow with burgundy red. There is a touch of dark purple in this color, too, so it suddenly looks as if some mythical giant had flung down his carpets to walk on. There is, as of now, one special bog on the way to Hyannis that pricks my eyelids with tears. It is in a depression with the land sloping gently down to where it spreads, and it takes all my stamina to bear the richness of the wine-dark beauty.

The first sight of land itself must have affected the Pilgrims in the same way. But they were starving and half-ill and facing a desperate struggle. I can drive home and get back to normal living by running the dustmop, which is humdrum enough to calm anyone down.

When winter comes, the bogs will be small lakes strung like fresh-water pearls on the Cape's bosom. Then bogs are flooded by pumping plants by way of irrigation ditches.

There they are, in the depths, like enchanted maidens waiting for the Prince of Spring—I don't know why everything about cranberry bogs makes me sentimental. So I must be realistic and wonder why this particular land plant can survive under water so long?

April is associated with freshening up, cleaning, getting paint jobs done before the midges come to help. Later there are the greenflies. I am always reminded about now of Mr. Anslow, our painter for years. The last time he came, he said he had time enough to "do" the living room and it was all arranged. He was then around eighty, a firm, rugged-faced man with the accent that cannot be reproduced.

He came over the night before, bringing his truck, and stood in the middle of the living-room floor looking at the walls, the color of bitter chocolate.

"Well," he said, "can't paint for you after all."

"Oh, why? Why not? Are you sick?"

"Nope," he said, "don't like that color."

I knew how he felt because brown is not my favorite color either. But this was chosen by our very dear friend Steve, who is a decorator, and he spent much thought on what background color was best for the intense light of a shore house with two walls almost all glass. Also he chose the brown to show off the ancient soft-pine dough chest, the lazy Susan, the harvest table and the Shaker sewing table.

But to Mr. Anslow it was still dark brown and he said goodbye!

Oddly enough, this is one reason people love the Cape. Cape Codders can be exasperating in a very special way, but they are never impersonal. They *care*, one way or another. We had a dreadful time, at that late date, replacing Mr. Anslow but we admired him nonetheless.

The characteristic that inlanders find hard to adjust to in the true Cape Codders is their general tendency to say Yes sometimes when they do not mean it at all. I have been inconvenienced myself by this but there must be some Cape blood in me from my ancestors, for I also feel it is MORE POLITE to say Yes than No. I've had this difficulty all of my life. *No* seems unkind. It is a rejection, any way you look at it. *Yes* is a sunny word.

The inland way of looking at life, so far as my years there go, is that a good flat No is something stable and honorable. For electricians, plumbers, treemen, painters, paperhangers —any professional man does not hesitate to say, "I'm sorry, I'm too busy, can't take on another job."

On-Cape, the voice with that endearing accent (I practice it at night with no result) says, "Well, I have some ahdahs ahead but I might make it around next Tuesday."

You feel better and he has not hurt your feelings. Six weeks later you may not be so relaxed.

But the basic lesson of the Cape is invaluable. Almost all of us who come across the bridge are tense, overwhelmed with schedules, full of guilt if anything is left undone. It is what Jill used to call the teeth-grinding syndrome.

Slowly for some, faster for others, the Cape philosophy gets into the bones. The high-geared retired vice-president will wave a casual hand and say, "Well, someday Mr. S will turn up—when fishing season is over."

As for me, having lived with deadlines for years, I now look out at the lawn and think it may get mowed before July. I can live, eat, work, listen to records, visit with friends, play with my Abyssinian kitten, go to watch the sunset at Rock Harbor whether that lawn *ever* gets mowed. I can just wade through the long grass.

In short, things fall into a perspective on the Cape that is impossible inland. At Stillmeadow, if the lawn doesn't get mowed, my son-in-law comes clear out from New York City to mow it. That is the way we operate inland.

I suppose what I am trying to express is that I think the Cape way is better, even when it leaves me with furnace trouble as I wait for Willie Gallant. I do have the best of two worlds, as the saying goes, for inland my Art Olsen will come at four in the morning when it is twenty below zero and the furnace gives a dismal moan and stops. On the Cape, my furnace gets "fitted in," but the mass building going on means that Willie Gallant hardly has time to sleep, so this doesn't belong, actually, with my premise except if I see Willie at the post office and he flashes that dark handsome smile at me, he says, yes he does, "I'll get around next Tuesday to clean your furnace!"

April slides into May and there is no way of mapping the moment May begins. There is a softening of outline in nature and even when the broadcaster advises the bogs should be flooded at night, noon is warm and the mockingbird sings away at the feeder.

May on Cape Cod is the year at its gayest. There is a passion of blooming. Gardens are gold with Baskets of Gold, purple with pansies, and countless flowers in blossom that I never identify. The Cape lilacs begin in mid-May to open their dark purple spikes. They are richer in color than inland, so they must like the salt air and thin soil. Before they are fully open, they actually look black.

Lilacs belong with old houses. At Stillmeadow the lilacs now climb as high as the roof. I have no idea how old they are. But a former owner had a hatred of lilacs and cut them all down. Up from the ravaged roots came new shoots and those lilacs reasserted their birthright.

Now on the Cape I notice the oldest saltboxes almost al-

ways have lilac hedges or masses of lilacs around the back
door or leaning over what once was probably a fish shed. On
some winding, untroubled roads lilacs mark the place where a
house once stood and makes a fragrant memorial.

Margaret Stanger and I plan to go to Chatham when the lilacs are at their peak and leave a bouquet at the grave of the
doctor who is buried outside of town by the roadside. It is a
sad story. During the smallpox plague in 1765–66, Dr. Lord
cared for everyone in Chatham, working day and night.
Eventually he, of course, caught the fatal disease. When he
died the inhabitants would not have him buried in the cemetery, in case of infection from his casket, I suppose. He was
buried hastily way out at the side of an untraveled road.

Now the gravestone is barely visible as the wildflowers and
grasses grow around it. Probably few see it on the way to the
Chatham airport. Margaret has been taking a Memorial Day
bouquet to the spot for a long time. It gives me sobering
thoughts, such as that when we criticize our own generation
we might remember cruelty and stupidity were not invented
in our time!

The oddest fact is that all of Dr. Lord's patients presumably were fit to be interred in hallowed ground. But the man
who gave his life for them was not!

On the way to absorb a Rock Harbor sunset, I passed the
beach plums along the meadow-edge of Rock Harbor Road.
They were just coming into full bloom and they are the real
music of May. The flowers are close-set on charcoal branches
and the bushes themselves are graceful as a ballet dancer. The
blooming is whiter than white until the end of it when the
whole bush turns a soft Victorian shade of pink and then ebbs
to cinnamon.

The Orleans garden specialist, who writes a charming col-

umn for the *Oracle* called "The Gal Next Door," has stated
that transplanting beach plums is almost impossible. But she
strewed ripe beach plums liberally around her garden border
and they rooted themselves and produced a nice windbreak
of beach plums and a snowdrift of bloom.

This brings me to the dangerous assumption that wildlings
on the Cape seldom transplant because, possibly, they have
the type of root systems that cannot be disturbed. Inland, in
thick rich soil, you can shovel up almost anything without
upsetting it, but our efforts to transplant those few cranberries from sand slopes I cannot call exactly a triumph.

When the beach plums are ripe, I shall get some and try
Janet's plan.

The shadblow this year coincided with the beach plum.
This has a thinner stitching of white blossoms on a rangier
bush. The flowering crab and the Japanese cherries the town
planted under the aegis of Ladybird also are in bloom. I re-
gret to say I do not feel they fit the Cape and have an artificial appearance, while the old apple trees, the pear trees, the
tulip trees seem to belong.

The main town talk now is when is it safe to put out the
geraniums. This is a VERY controversial subject. Bill Wildman, the quiet, tall man at Miss Rogers' Flower Shop (it will
always be called Miss Rogers' Flower Shop no matter who
owns it, I am glad to say), says May fifteenth is the earliest
possible date.

Someone came to call on me this week and said in surprise,
"Where did you get those lovely geraniums?"

"Miss Rogers' Flower Shop."

"But he wouldn't sell me any!"

"Well, last year by the time I got down for them they
were all gone. So I drove down back by the greenhouse yes-

terday and waited until the new girl came over and Bill was busy. I bought a carton full of the loveliest pink and Bob Chandler put them in the urns and they are fine so far."

Frost *can* come up to the fifteenth quite easily but it hasn't so far.

I have seldom known anyone who could create a bouquet as lovely as Bill Wildman's. His flowers always look comfortable and seem to belong as he arranges them. They always last longer than they have any right to. But I do have a feeling that he only wants to be with his flowers and plants and that people are a nuisance. I speak to him timidly.

A successful bouquet is really a flower arrangement, but should not advertise the fact. Some of the professional ones leave me quite frigid. I can see every single technical detail since I learned a lot when I wrote my two books on flower arranging and studied it for several years. But nothing that has to do with flowers should be mechanical.

My neighbor Kay often pops over with a small bouquet —perhaps three or five small wildflowers in a green-glass ink bottle. A tiny spray of pine or honeysuckle gives them companionship and the effect is charming. She has a natural gift for making do with any material around, spring, summer, winter.

My Scotch broom is penciling out pale lemon needle-slender spikes and, alas, I am no good at making bouquets with it. It just sprays out and hangs in mid-air and nothing goes with it. But this week I shall consult Kay. She may find a piece of driftwood and drill a hole in it and plant a few spikes in the gray and have a masterpiece!

In a world of blossoming, Rock Harbor is serene. But shadows of history linger here. In 1810, the British used to anchor off Defiance Lane and the officers walked to the stately pillared Inn which is now the home of my dear friend

Helen Beals. The old Inn sign is now buried so deep in one of the great branches of the front elm that nobody can tell what the name was. Helen calls the place Lilac Farm.

Packets landed at Rock Harbor from Plymouth, Boston, Salem and the Maritime Provinces. Gentlemen and lady travelers had to walk to the Inn from the landing to be entertained. But the serenity did not last, for Britain had already begun to seize American ships and impress the sailors she needed to have in her blockade of France. At the end of 1810 she had seized four thousand American sailors and two-thirds were impressed—which is an odd way of phrasing it!

Then she began to arm Indians for a border invasion and by 1814 burned Washington. On December 19, 1814, the Orleans militia repulsed a British landing from the H.M.S. *Newcastle*, which was intent on burning, as they put it, all the vessels and the whole village.

It is hard to think of the village militia with no decent firearms and no training repulsing a naval ship from England, and somehow it brings a lump to the throat to think of the women and children hidden behind barred doors, listening to the sound of the guns at Rock Harbor.

The elegant British officers never came to the Inn again. But often as I sit in what must have been the gentlemen's parlor where the fire burned bright on the ancient hearth and hot rum was at hand, I feel a sense of the past which is tangible. The house is full of presences, happy, relaxed ones. I think the officers who loved the Inn would have hesitated to put the torches to it!

And on that dark December day, some of them must have wondered why this war was going on—as all men wonder about all wars.

Some of the British undoubtedly came from the same places in England as the original Orleans settlers. Some of them had relatives buried in the same cemeteries and the basic tie of race kinship could not be wiped out. I wonder when, in the history of the world, man became the only creature to kill his own kind, destroy his own brother.

A few British soldiers were buried in one of the old cemeteries farther toward the Cape tip but I do not think any were laid to rest in Orleans. But the Cape is full of ghosts.

On these shining mornings, I have my breakfast tray by the big window. I can look across Mill Pond to the landing and see where the tide-water grist mill stood in 1700. Some of the foundation is still there. Timothy Cole and Lewis Doane operated it and the sloping road to the landing must have been a busy place. Across the inlet, the largest salt evaporation operation in town was run. It occupied one thousand feet along Robert's Cove.

Salt, I reflect, has been a basic need of man, not to mention wildlife—some of whom will chew up oars to get a lick of salt from the oarsman's sweaty hands. The salt block we keep at Stillmeadow for deer, chucks, coons and whoever needs it, melts away fast. Now, salty as my sea water is, it would be a deadly chore to evaporate it to get enough salt to use. The water in the early days was pumped into long vats and the sun gradually evaporated enough moisture to leave a residue of the precious product.

I shake my seasoned salt and seasoned pepper on my soft-boiled egg and know I may have all I want just by going to Ellis' market in town. Even ordinary salt nowadays pours free, as the ads say. When I was a child, salt would cake and be dug out of the salt jar with a spoon. Peppercorns were poured in a small grinder and came out in bits and granules. The spicy dark smell filled the kitchen.

Spices and pepper and tea and countless necessities came to the Cape only by frigate. But the Cape Codders made do.

Top: View from author's living room. (*John Schram*)

Bottom: Desk at far end of study. (*John Schram*)

The Indian corn and squash were available. The early reports all say "fish teemed" in ponds, lakes and the sea. Lobsters and shellfish were easy to take. Wild turkeys flew over (and how tough they must have been).

Perhaps the people ate wild blackberries.

The Indians had discovered the dark sap that ran down the maples could become a sweet by boiling. Otherwise sweet was scarce unless a few men found bee trees with honey and braved the bee stings without masks or nets.

Then there was the cod. Someone who should have been immortalized dreamed up a way to dry and salt it. It was, I am told, dried on racks along the beaches and did make a considerable smell as it dried.

But the era of creamed codfish or codfish cakes was born. For winter morning breakfasts what is better than a few tiny crisp codfish cakes with a twist of lemon peel, a spoonful of beach plum jelly on the side and hot coffee?

It is no wonder the first man who began to think more or less like a man worshiped the sun. The sun was the source of heat and light and when it shone, things grew and ripened. And could be preserved.

Few people any more make sun-dried strawberry preserves, I imagine. Mama used to spread the richest, ripest strawberries on a rack covered with fine muslin. This was put in the back yard and a layer of mosquito netting tacked over. Gradually the sun blackened the berries as they dried. I don't know the end of the process, since at that time my interest in cooking and/or preserving was more than limited. It did not exist.

But the strawberry preserves that resulted were sweeter than any honey Hybla ever had.

By the time the Cape Codders were established, fireplaces were used for cooking. But a link with prehistoric man per-

sisted and still does, fortunately. Before man had any iron or
pottery cooking utensils, he found if he lined a pit with
stones preheated by fire and then poured water in the pit, he
could drop grain in to make a mash or gruel.

So today on Cape Cod we have the clambake, the peak of
delicious eating. Hot stones are set in a sand pit and sea
grasses tossed on. The shellfish go in and the juices of the sea
grass steam them. Some clambakes have lobsters and corn in
the husk and clams, and when you finish you plan a day of
milk toast to follow! If Portuguese bread is also served, I am
too busy sopping up juices to converse.

But what pleases me most is the thought that this is a heritage from prehistory so that pit cooking today links us to the
unimaginable past.

Incidentally, the first time we went to a Firemen's lobster
dinner at Eastham, I became educated about eating lobsters.
These were big ruddy lobsters dripping with rich juice. They
were served on paper plates at the long outdoor trestle tables.
I was fresh from inland and had always approached a lobster
with five instruments plus a massive pair of lobster shears and
a lapful of paper napkins.

Now I had a lobster and nothing else. My neighbor at the
table was a weathered sea-blue-eyed Cape Codder and he
said, "I think good eating."

He picked up his lobster and twisted it. Then he made a
couple of more moves with his square sun-browned hands. In
all, it took him five manipulations while I watched helplessly.
He did not even lose ANY juice!

Like most Cape Codders (there are some exceptions) he
was sorry for an ignorant inlander and in five more twists
had my own lobster ready to eat without even a fork. As we
sucked the last bit of meat from our respective lobsters, we
agreed it was a good party.

This particular May struck a note of disaster in Orleans. At first in the post office, I met Helen Beals who whispered in my ear, "Have you heard about Ellis's?"

"It can't have burned down," I said, "I've just been there for some fresh mushrooms."

"Mr. Ellis has sold," said Helen.

"He can't have! This is one disaster we cannot bear in Orleans," I said. "Ellis is the heart of the town, the center of everything. We can't live without Ellis' market."

"A man from across the bridge has bought it," said Helen, firmly.

Outside I met two more friends. "Have you heard?" they said in unison.

An air of Gothic gloom pervaded every place in town.

So when I went to a coffee party at Eleanor Luscomb's, I tried to explain to her guest from inland. I found it difficult, and still do, to express the meaning of this small, crowded country store in our lives. It summed up the past friendliness of a less-pressured age. It represented something stable in an age of instability. At Ellis's one was not a number but a person.

For instance when I first went in this spring, Sarah Parent greeted me at the counter.

"Your cousin is heayr," she said. "Have you seen him?"

"No, I just got here," I told her.

"They came four days ago," Sarah said, "and they will be heayr until the first of next week. They have a lot of work to do out on Barley Neck Road."

Last summer I went in for one of the special steaks and Sarah said, "Your two friends Vincent and George from New Yohk City just came in this afternoon and they are in Truro. They will phone you tonight."

So when the phone rang that night, I said, "Welcome to Cape Cod, George. Sarah said you had arrived."

"We stopped in on our way to Truro to see everyone at Ellis's," said George. "Of course we never buy anything anywhere else. There is no atmosphere like Ellis's."

Mr. Ellis, who has owned the store ever since we began coming to the Cape, and I think his father owned it before him, is a strong, agile man with the Cape sea-colored eyes and bronzed skin. There are legends about him as to how many thousands of dollars he lets ride on the books in a poor fishing season, or how often he forgets to send bills when families are in trouble. If he denied this, nobody would pay any attention.

He is loved, as few big businessmen ever are, that I do know.

In the store, which is small, confused, narrow-aisled, it is sometimes impossible to move one step forward. But it doesn't matter because you visit with the person next to you while you stand there. Sarah's husband, Gordon, runs back and forth wearing his straw hat and helping find missing items for customers. Gordon has his own filing system for the merchandise, and it is not like the supermarkets with their impersonal listings on huge placards. Gordon files things according to where he thinks they should be and his mind is his own computer.

Marge Eugley is at the counter and she is a lovely, quiet, feminine young woman with a mind like a steel trap. Her voice is gentle and her smile shy and she reminds me of a bouquet of violets picked in a meadow. Here again we are rested from the miniskirts and false eyelashes and teased hair. Two more women are there who are a pleasure to visit with and make a point of helping weigh the tomatoes (I cannot weigh anything on one of those scales—it comes out a ton and a half).

The meat cutters, as we call them still, are deft, patient with customers who spend thirty minutes choosing between chops. Nobody has to be more patient than a butcher, as I already have noted in Southbury, Connecticut.

Down the years, Ellis has delivered twice a week and this is a special boon to anyone who cannot lug huge bags of groceries (I cannot). On Monday and Thursday mornings, Sarah or Marge would take my ahdah. During the summer, a boy brings the groceries but when things are tight, Mr. Ellis himself drives up in the stocky truck. The frozen things are *put in the freezer* if I am not in. Butter and eggs are tucked in the lower part of the refrigerator. Chicken and chops go on the top shelf.

The boy who delivered last season went off to the navy, as it figures on Cape Cod. His grandmother kept me up with where he was, as she is in the store. When he had a leave, he came to see me, and the only reason I knew him was that he had discarded his uniform and was wearing the same green and purple shirt he wore during the summer. But he had grown a couple of inches and his hair was cropped like a mowed lawn.

How else can I describe Ellis's? When the children were here last August, Connie, my daughter, went into the market to get some steaks for the ten- and eight-year-old granddaughters. She came home, apologetic and worried. She said when she asked for thin steaks, the look she got was of complete disbelief.

"The worst of it was, Mamma," she said, "they knew I was *your* daughter. I've disgraced you. I tried to say it was just for the girls—they won't eat anything thick—but I don't know!"

Perhaps I can sum this loss up by saying we live in an age when there is almost nothing personal left. We are ciphers and statistics, and computers figure for us. The basic human need to be an individual is forgotten.

Sometimes in the confusion of an overcrowded store with

summer people and cartons of orders all over the back room, things went wrong. I once got Orin Tovrov's order when they were having a party.

Tovrov and Taber sound much alike and we live near each other. But I phoned Midge Tovrov and there was no problem at all. We swapped groceries.

Today Mr. Ellis came with my order, since the new regime is not yet settled in. I tried to express my feeling about Ellis's going. I cannot say why anyone who spends a lifetime with words has times when there just are none!

Mr. Ellis stood a minute looking at the view, a scudding cloudy Mill Pond this day, and speaking to Amber, who was eating grass.

"Well," he said, "there comes a time. I thought my son might take over but he is doing so well in his business it would have been a mistake for him. The new owner is a nice young man."

"If he changes the store," I said, "he will go bankrupt."

He smiled. "Now," he said, "I know you have a little trouble getting around." (I have arthritis and use a cane for steps.) "I want to tell you if you ever need anything too heavy for you to lug, you give me a ring and I'll bring it out—even if I *don't* work there any more."

I carried Amber back in the house and took off her harness and sat watching the Mill Pond turn to apricot and I thought about what really gives life value. What gives value is not a spectacular deed or achievement. What is important is daily, and it may not be world-shaking—but I wonder whether it wouldn't be if it were multiplied?

If all of us cared enough for our fellow man—well, perhaps someday we shall.

Meanwhile my heart is still aching at the idea of Ellis's changing—who wants all the soups in one area? We do not want the vegetables suffocated in plastic. And I want to exchange recipes with Marge and Sarah and the rest of them.

I want someone at the counter to ask how my kitten is and not just push a button for the bill.

I kept the big card from the market that signified the end of an era: *Notice—beginning May 5th there will be one delivery a week and orders must be called in before one P.M.*

As a recipe for how not to make friends, I thought this was worth saving. With Amber's wide-eyed help, I revised it: *Dear Customer—We expect Ellis' market to continue the same type of service you have been used to. However, due to the press of business during the season, we regretfully must limit deliveries to one a week. Also the staff can no longer call the customers for orders. With best wishes . . .*

A pleasant change from this was when I went to Beth Bishop's, the elegant dress shop. My method of shopping for clothes may be unique. I sit down and my dear friend Millie flies around choosing things that will be right for me. Her frequent remark is, "This is lovely but it doesn't *do* anything for you." I used to ask why, but now I know better. Millie explained that my neck is short, my shoulders too square, my frame too stocky.

This day Millie was laid up with one of those gregarious viruses so I was shopping alone, but Dorothea Webb was at Beth's and found just what she and Millie would both feel suitable for me. Then Beth Bishop came in and broke the news that she had sold the shop.

"Now don't turn pale," she said. "I want you to meet the new owner, Mrs. Carey . . . ," and she bustled off and came back with the new owner, one of those quiet slim women who always remind me of English country gardens. They are always casually dressed in soft browns or beige or lime green (this is rare) and their shoes have no high heels.

"I want to assure you," said Mrs. C. in a soft voice, "that nothing will be changed. Nothing at all will be changed. This

will be exactly the way it has always been and Dorothea
Webb and the other girls will help you whenever you need
help."

"And I am staying on until August so we can shop together," added Beth.

Much as I dislike change, I felt reassured about this one, especially when Mrs. C. said, "It will be called Beth Bishop's as
usual."

A driving Sou'wester is sheeting Mill Pond with rain. This
rain goes in great waves like smoke and the effect is strange
and disquieting. The wind is so strong I cannot open the door
at the front of the house, it has the violence of an autumn
storm. My newly washed windows will be paved with salt.

So when I turned on the radio, the weather report for
Plymouth, Cape Cod and the offshore islands was cloudy,
with showers, this afternoon. I was, as always, tempted to call
up the station and suggest someone drive out and look at the
weather.

Tomorrow this rain will be out over the Atlantic, which is
my own weather report. The three-day storms begin with a
blacker sky over the water and high tides foam in to the
beach grass. The sound of the wind is wilder.

This is hard weather for people opening cottages. One
family arrived and found the furnace up to its neck in water
from a winter leak. Another found that various wild creatures had worked in through the kitchen screen door. The
truth is no cottage or house should be left all winter with nobody to check on it. There are on the Cape a number of
firms who do nothing but check houses. Many lucky people
have neighbors who care. Millie and Ed drop in regularly at
my house and a good many disasters have been avoided. One
window leak can soak the best rug in the house.

Tomorrow will be fair and crystalline and every leaf polished. The wild roses are uncurling more leaflets and the maples by the small pond will look as if every one of their leaves had been edged with pinking shears.

And Amber can nibble fresh grass when we go outdoors!

As the cars begin coming to the narrow land, it is a rising tide all its own. Some Cape people believe the weight of tourists will eventually cause the whole Cape to sink beneath the ocean, particularly with so much building expansion to add weight.

This is usually qualified by the statement, "Of course, some of my best friends are summer people!"

I reflect about this as the town grows more crowded and the serenity, we must face, is gone until after Labor Day. The truth is you cannot pack thousands of extra human beings in a limited area and not have problems.

The tourist revenue is a major item in Cape economy but comes at a high price sometimes. Renting cottages is rather like buying tickets to sweepstakes. I have two examples I think of. My dear friends Helen and Vicky rent a nearby cottage. They take care of the garden, water the lawn, replace even a broken juice glass and buy whatever small items they think would add to the cottage. Several days before they leave, they have the rugs cleaned, polish the floors, defrost the refrigerator, clean the fireplace. Guests who go over must walk on newspapers not to bring any sand in!

Then last summer I went over to Barbara Lovely's and found her in tears. She is not a crying woman, any more than I am, but she had rented a cottage for someone and the tenants were practically demolishing it, bit by bit. They had a lease and there they were. When they left, the house had to be done over.

I do not know whether they do this, but I would think the realtors who work so hard and are so conscientious might well have a blackball list to protect the rental properties.

One more reminiscence I have about rents. A family I knew rented their charming house just once to a very wealthy and elegant off-Cape—let me call her Mrs. Van Buren because that is an elegant name. They did this really as a favor for mutual friends, as they were going to Colorado for a visit and thought the house would be better off in good hands. They left everything, linen, stocked shelves, soaps, detergents . . .

The house was immaculate when they got back, not a toothpick out of place in the cocktail canapé tray. My friend was upset because there was no sign of life having gone on —but she is a sentimental woman. Not a posy in the window—not a small present for the hostess. But she did find, finally, a twenty-five-cent tea strainer in the kitchen drawer and went around happily telling us all there was a house present after all!

A month later Mrs. Van Buren stopped by to say she had forgotten her tea strainer and she took it with her!

This just reinforces my opinion that people take themselves into any situation they go into.

Perhaps one of the happiest days of my life was when I heard Sarah explaining at Ellis' market that Mrs. Taber had to go away part of the year but was not a summer person really. She had to go back to Connecticut to the fahm but she really belongs hyeh.

And I note that with Helen and Vicky the townspeople say it is such a pity they have to go to New Jersey to teach all year—they have to earn a living.

"And do you know," they add, in wonder, "they are as good drivers as you could ever find—and from New Jersey!"

The sorrowful problem of hippies is beginning early this year. A friend in Eastham who lives off the main road in a remodeled barn reported that at 9:30 at night in the rain, two bedraggled hippies knocked on the door. They wanted to know where the nearest campsite was. They were young teens, a boy and girl, with shabby knapsacks. The night, being May, was around 50 degrees.

My friend Ted has two prekindergarten babies and he and his wife were ready for bed. He felt, rightly, he could not let the hippies in. He thought they wandered off toward the Coast Guard beach and slept in the lee of a dune (against the law).

Last summer I went to the post office for the mail as usual and chose an off hour when I might conceivably park. On the debris-strewn sidewalk a slender, long-haired blonde girl was propped up against the post office wall. She had a young and defenseless face and she was on a trip without a return ticket, I thought. I spoke to her but she could not answer and I could not lift her in the car to take her to my doctor. But someone had phoned the police—God bless them—

This was the first experience I had had with a hippie and it left a deep mark.

When I got home I had my first fan letter from a hippie —such a confused and touching two-page outpouring of desires and longings and anxieties. And she signed it *Love and Peace Rhonda*. With no address. I think the main problem with all of these—or most—is just that—no address. I could not even make anything of the postmark, for the post office, as usual, had stamped over it three times.

My preparation for the summer invasion is to make one of my futile efforts to be organized. I make lists and lose them. I go through the house, as I do at Stillmeadow, and write down everything that is needed. Then it takes some time to interpret *B T* later on. *N P* works out to new pillows. *B T* means new bathroom trays for the top of the toilet tanks.

By mid-May I go to Snow's for manuscript envelopes, Pentels, a trowel and putty knife and so on. At the drugstore I buy all the Rxs I shall need for the season (once nearly giving Slim Lovely a nervous collapse because he knew I could NOT have taken a WHOLE bottle of whatever it was, that would be dangerous). I explained I emptied the bottle in a soup bowl but *would* need a refill by August.

All things needing cleaning go to Acme where two warm-hearted girls lug the stuff in for me.

Meanwhile I have been to the dentist for a prophylaxis, as he calls it. My interpretation is that Lucy Doe tries her hardest to find just one small cavity SOMEWHERE. I go with Millie to South Harwich to Dr. Anne, the podiatrist, just to be sure my feet are in A-1 shape as long as I don't give in to high heels (I only did during courtship days).

Then Amber and I go to Kim Schneider, the veterinarian, which we did this morning. Already, on May 22nd, his office was crowded with bumbling big puppies and small nervous no-name darlings. He had not seen Amber since I left the Cape for Connecticut last fall and he said, "Well, Amberino, how did you make out this winter?"

He is the only person to call her Amberino and it is a term of endearment although she did NOT want her mouth examined and her throat looked at and said so with bells on. To a cat, a mouth is the truly private place. I believe, in my own amateur's way, that a kitten's mouth does not open wide easily—mine never has either since I had a jaw infection in childhood. My dentist has a hard time getting my mouth open wide enough to fill a pinpoint cavity.

Kim has a light and easy way of speaking to animals with never a hint of criticism or of disciplinary tones. George Whitney, in New Haven, has the same way of speech and I found it also in Dr. Bernstein in Yarmouth. I thought this was the way veterinarians were.

But I had occasion to go, in an emergency, to a good veterinarian when I was somewhere else some time ago and I learned a good deal. This doctor knew exactly what he was doing but he was not feeling any empathy with the patient. He was not really shouting but almost, and grabbing, and red in the face. The patient was trying to climb the walls and so was its owner. It was a shattering experience.

The Rx was perfect, but the treatment was an emotional crisis.

I told Kim this season I was checking in before the invasion—and he said he projected going to Europe for a while this August so he could avoid Taunton (the hospital nearest for mental breakdowns).

We talked a bit about Holly. The difference between an Irish and many other dogs, except cockers, is a complete acceptance that what you are pushing down their necks is the thing to do. The tail wags all the time in a forgiving way as they choke on a nasty pill. Cockers gag but keep wagging. Cats forgive you afterward.

When we got home, Amber flew into my lap and purred and rubbed and kneaded her paws indicating that I *was* finally FORGIVEN for putting her in the carrier and taking her all the way to Eastham and letting that man (whom she really does cotton to) poke in her mouth and scrape her teeth. She forgave me in a regal production.

Then she gave herself a good bath and settled down by the typewriter to work the keys with me and try to catch the carriage.

The greens of May are a whole color palette in themselves. I think it would be enough to give a painter a nervous breakdown if he tried to reproduce them. I lose count when I try to make a list of the shadings from the green-gold fountains of the willows to the polished inky-green of

Holly, shown here as a puppy, found seagull watching from the picture windows at Still Cove a daylong preoccupation.

the wild rosebushes. The tender aqua of the fruit trees contrasts with the black-green of the cedars and jack pines.

But there are really countless other tones in bush and marsh and in the end I try to rest from the excitement by going to Rock Harbor to look at sand. But the shadings of the marsh grasses and the colors in the sand itself have their own enchantment.

Sand is not one color either. A handful of sand represents the action of ages on varying rock and it glitters if you look closely, with a rainbow of delicate hues. At a distance, it may appear a tawny shining expanse, but the rock that was ground up to make it has left a signature. Also, of course, there is much pulverized shell in it as the endless tides sweep in and out on nature's eternal business.

Man's idea of precious stones is strange. There are pinky mauve and pearly pebbles on Cape beaches that have not yet been ground into the shingle and are lovely to feel and to look at. They would make a good setting by Tiffany except they are picked up by amateurs who like them and are not exported from some far-off country and are not so RARE as to be like black diamonds. They are available to you and me.

A few artists have, of late, been making bracelets and pins and earrings of Cape stones as well as shells and they have more appeal to me than diamonds because they are an extra link with the mystery of the sea.

My song sparrow continues to be an astonishment to me. I have no way of knowing whether this is the same one who has nested in the same cedar for four or five years or is a descendant, since the life tenure of small songbirds seems to be a debatable question among ornithologists. It is easy to measure the life span of a bird in captivity where you can watch it, but a migrant songster seems difficult. How many succumb to adverse weather too young, or to hawks or hungry cats, or fly into picture windows—well, anyway for five years at least I have had a song sparrow who acts as if he had been here for a decade. He sits on the same tip of the same cedar, he nests in the same small space in the midst of the thicket. He flies to the birdbath at the same hour.

And he sings! Yesterday morning at five, I got up to turn the furnace on. This is that kind of May. The small vibrant bird with the black dot on his chest was up and singing. He sang madly while I tried to get a little more sleep and I felt humiliated because I was not also up and singing at that hour, but was wondering whether I would make it one more time (my usual morning feeling). The burst of song was bigger than his whole tiny body.

He was still singing while I had my coffee and grapefruit and Amber had her junior lamb with broth. Then I followed the usual routine, off for the mail, errands, back to work. By three in the afternoon I was rolling a fresh sheet of paper in the typewriter, hampered by Amber's helping paws, when I realized that song sparrow was, yes, SINGING!

So I watched the clock as I got supper—lamb chops, fresh asparagus and broiled mushrooms (one chop for Amber, plus the tips of the asparagus plus the tenderest mushroom). The news came on with all the world devastation pinpointed by the broadcasters. Then I cleaned up the kitchen and came back in the living room at eight o'clock.

The song sparrow was *still* whittling away at the scale. I do not know of anything more qualified to make a human being feel inferior. I opened the door gently and spoke to this morsel swaying on the top twig in a stiff sea breeze.

"You are an inspiration," I said, "but I can't live up to you."

I have said before that I am sure the experts are right that birds do not sing because they are happy but to establish their right to their own territory (they have no guns to fire off).

Nevertheless, the song of a bird has a heart-lifting effect which no roar of a gun could ever have. And I am romantic enough to think the silvery syllables of a bird song must make the producers satisfied, and of course does not result in a casualty list.

The 23rd of May I marked off on the calendar, for my first rosy purple finch came to the birdbath and the mockingbird was tipping around in the tall grass. The finches do not often come right on the beach property but prefer it at Mrs. Luscomb's, which is sheltered, as do the towhees and what we used to call wild canaries.

I drive five miles an hour when I go for the mail because the main thing about a young quail is that he or she cannot decide which way to go. When they are very small, they follow the parents in a dither and there is always at least one that can barely make it to keep up. Quail, young or old, move with a jerky pushing of the head as if to provide motor power to keep the rather awkward bodies mobile. They have trouble getting up in the air and always seem to be off-balance for the first few wingspreads.

There are so many on my land that I feel I might walk on them if I were not careful. I stop the motor in the car and wait while they run back and forth from one side of the road to the other, never really making up their minds. Finally they plunge into the thicket at one side, emerge with a great flurry and rush to the other side.

There is no bird more endearing, for they seem to reflect the dilemma of us all. I, too, have trouble deciding which side of a road I should be on—especially when it comes to politics or world affairs or even mundane things like having chicken again for dinner.

Quail are peculiarly helpless and innocent birds and it must take a special killer instinct to make it possible to mow them down as they have been in the past. My friend Margaret

Stanger spent some time with Robert, the Quail, and found the intelligence and feeling rated very high—and she is a psychologist used to estimating I.Q.s.

When a covey of young quail go across the yard, Amber is interested, but as long as they do not fly she just watches from the picture window. The seagulls that wheel past the windows and the hawk at dusk and the blackbirds who sit on the split-rail fence singing *okalee-okalee* for hours, these cause her to grind her teeth in a strange way and make a chittering sound I have tried to describe before.

But her language and mine are mutually understandable. Visitors sometimes look at me oddly when I say, "Amber is asking for a snack and says she is tired of beef and would like lamb."

Or at night, when the moon is out, I may jump up while visitors are discussing the political situation and say, "Amber says there is a skunk on the steps."

We have a few strange cats who come around and there is a special vocabulary for them, too. This involves a swelling of the fur on the rear and a thrashing of tail. And a low rolling sound from deep in the throat.

For such a small fragile person, Amber is possessed of the strength of ten. A large monster-sized dog may come in and Amber swells and swells and swells and hisses and stands on tiptoe, whiskers quivering. No hiding for her under the bed or behind the television set.

When she is persuaded this is a nice friendly boy, she establishes a status quo by casually washing her hind legs. Then polishing her ears. Most of the visiting dogs stay in a corner respectfully. After they leave, Amber looks helpless and frail again, no fiercer than a wood violet!

I read last night about a couple in the West who have a house built on a rotating steel shaft so that they can turn it in whichever direction they feel like. It is, of course, circular but the architect husband has managed to make it look less like a pie than you would think.

My reaction was to get in the car and drive along Bridge Road, down Monument Road, along Barley Neck, past Minister's Prim and then home by Ruggles Road where my favorite half-house stands.

The true Cape Cod house is as close to perfection as possible. The shape was saltbox in the earliest version, fitted snugly to the ground and with small-paned windows to withstand the winter gales. In my part of Connecticut the steep roofs also were prevalent but this must have been to shed the tons of snow in winter. Flat roofs would not survive it. Since snow is rather rare on the Cape, I think the steepness there was to allow the Nor'easters to hit with full fury without ripping off roofs. Also I am reminded the Cape Codders were fine boat-builders, and the bow of a Cape fishing boat has somewhat the same shape when it lies beached on the sands.

Later the Georgian houses were popular, elegant with pillars and verandas, and many with widow's walks on the roofs. Sea captains who never sailed back to home port could presumably think of their wives keeping vigil endless hours from the widow's walks. They are rather small areas enclosed by waist-high fencing. My favorite of all is Whalewalk, a square white mansion with charcoal-colored shutters. Beyond it is a second one almost like it but not quite as lovely. The story is that two brothers built them for their wives and then sailed off captaining their whalers, probably hoping the wives would get along!

The advent of verandas coincides with more leisure, I feel sure. In the early houses, both inland and on-Cape, nobody ever thought of sitting in a rocking chair on a porch. Babies were rocked when they had colic but otherwise women had no idle moments.

Top: The Collins house, the oldest in Orleans. (*John Schram*)

Bottom: The Joshua Crosby house. (*John Schram*)

The half-house is my favorite. It is truly a half-house. It is the shape of the typical Cape house but is literally *just* half of a house. It has a door, sometimes at the right, sometimes at the left, and two windows in front. The earliest ones had no foundations but rested right on the ground, on the Cape sand (which may have prevented them from rotting).

They almost invariably are tucked in behind lilacs which often top the roofs. Cape ramblers bloom in the tiny door-yards, along with bleeding hearts, wood hyacinths and other plants with a bouquet of yesterday.

One legend is that wise fathers built them for marriageable daughters. Then the husbands could build the other half and the happy couple settle down to a life of hard work and many children. But if the daughter never married, she had the half-house to live in and was provided for.

This is a form of providing a dowry that I do not know of anywhere else and I admire the ingenuity of the fathers as well as their kind of matrimonial gamble!

Fortunately most people who buy half-houses do not ruin them by adding wings on each end. They tend, bless them, to put the additions in back where they are not visible as you drive by. It takes a stony heart to spoil a half-house for it has a fairy-tale look about it and the ghost of the lonely virgin who waited in it only adds a touch of nostalgia.

Dating the very ancient houses is usually a problem. Records were not kept well in the early times and frequently the town records were burned. Land sales were confused. The Cape is better off in this respect than my part of Connecticut.

I go by the Giles Hopkins homestead twice a day at least. Giles was born in England in 1610 and was a *Mayflower* passenger. In 1618 he settled in Orleans and died in 1690 and was buried in the Eastham Old Cove cemetery. He founded the Hopkins family on Cape Cod.

I feel sure the white house on the hill overlooking Town Cove may not be the first building on the site. But on this one piece of land Giles Hopkins began his family. I wonder whether he ever was homesick for England and if the struggle to live on the Narrow Land was rewarding? The freedom the Pilgrims came for did not follow since they soon became as regimented and didactic and rigid as their government back home.

Witchcraft came with them, too, although Salem was what might be called the witchcraft capital of the colonies. My own ancestors, the Mathers, especially the Reverend Cotton Mather, are always connected with persecution of the witches but a new scholar has now decided they weren't as black as they have been painted. In the end Cotton was influential in stopping the persecutions.

But looking at my own family, I may say the absolute sense of being right was still a dominant part of my father, his three brothers and the four sisters. Any deviation from the Mather right was a deadly sin. Compromise was not in my father's vocabulary, with all the Greek and Latin and Spanish he spoke!

I cannot picture any true Mather easygoing and tolerant. But they were interesting men, dedicated to learning always. One was the first native-born president of Harvard; another helped found Yale.

My favorite story of the Reverend Richard is his crossing from England in 1672 (I think that was his crossing). A terrible storm came up, the ship was about to founder, and Richard, in his full, flowing robe, stood clinging to a mast in the bow and wrestled with God. The storm, naturally, abated.

They were all handsome men and even the engravings in our genealogy cannot smudge the brilliance of the eyes (blue, of course) or the firm long upper lip and straight-bridged nose. The wigs were elegant but I know the hair underneath was a mop of reddish curls. Since my father looked so much like the first Mathers, I will guess they also had the fair skin and pink cheeks because if temperament can come down so undiluted, certainly skin tones may.

My reservations about Cotton have two bases. He once held his five-year-old daughter in his arms and pursued the subject of sin until she had fits. And there was the pirate affair. The pirates came to Cape Cod in 1717 on a spring day. The flagship was the *Whidaw*, with 23 guns and 130 men. The story is confused, but according to the legend, the deposed skipper of the *Whidah* (it is spelled both ways) threw a burning tarbarrel overboard and the helmsman, being drunk, followed the light and the ship went aground off Wellfleet.

The pirate treasure mysteriously vanished, but when Captain Southack from Boston came to investigate, 102 bodies were strewn on the beach.

Two of the other vessels managed to ride out the storm but the pirate vessel *Mary Anne* ran ashore on Pochet Island in Orleans, and seven pirates and some captured crewmen came ashore and celebrated at Crosby's tavern, captors and captured equally happy.

By the next noon, they were all captives, and the six practicing pirates taken to Boston and sentenced to death. Now Reverend Cotton Mather came to save their souls. They had to sit and listen, and possibly at moments they wondered whether any fate was not better than that!

I suspect this may have been the Reverend's main defeat, for several days later he stopped talking and simply escorted the pirates to the scaffold. My books report that one pirate went mad but the others sang hymns so perhaps the influence of my ancestor had some effect after all!

A good many ships lie buried off the Cape but real pirate treasure never seemed to be around when investigators came. The natives had not even heard a ship distress signal.

The lure of treasure is universal and even now some people

are looking for gold and jewel chests, and sometimes find Indian relics or bits of old masts and spars. A special treasure is
an ancient iron anchor which comes to grace some Cape Cod
garden. Then my friend Margaret Stanger has a harpoon
from the whaling days, which is mounted over the door to
the keeping room and, she points out proudly, still has dried
blood on the tip!

Whaling is a chapter in Cape history I try not to think of
often. Whale oil was essential and in 1712 the capture of a
sperm-oil whale by a Nantucket fisherman was an important
moment, and from 1820 to a short time before the Civil War
whalers cruised the seas, sometimes being gone three or four
years. When petroleum grew more available and the whales
decreased (anything exploited cannot last forever) the day of
the whaling ships was over, except for some commercial
whaling which involves explosives in the head of the har-
poons.

The whales were three to four tons in weight and could
crush a whaler to kindling if they hit head on. So it was a long
and bloody struggle. The whale can dive 3,000 feet and can
swim 20 knots. The harpoon at Margaret's stretches halfway
across the room, but it is hard to imagine it being buried to
the hilt in a thrashing monster. Naturally my sympathy
would be with the whale, quietly subsisting on plankton
sucked in as he swam by moving his tail back and forth. The
whale offspring are nursed, being mammals, and may nurse
even when weighing in at three tons!

Nowadays sometimes a young whale gets beached at
Truro or Wellfleet and no one knows why. A whale cannot
live if dehydrated, and dozens of youngsters and retirees will
spend day and night sluicing the gasping whale with buckets
of water with the hope of saving her life. But a few troubled
young ones who must destroy everything sneak out and cut
off pieces of skin for souvenirs when nobody is looking.

My friend Ivan Sandrof wrote about one of these whales

in the Worcester *Telegram* some summers ago, and I felt it should be required reading for all of us in this age.

This is the 25th of May and on the Cape we are faced with a dilemma, for this year for the second time we have two holidays—two Memorial Days. The new Massachusetts law arranging for holidays to be celebrated on Mondays, regardless of the date, in order to make long weekends, has been in operation without much success so far.

Tomorrow all stores will be closed for the first Memorial Day, but the banks and post office, which are federally run, will be open. Then on the real Memorial Day the second celebration occurs. Housewives are hard hit. At the market I was trying to get in some extras and so was everyone who didn't know when the next delivery might be.

I THINK there will be one parade tomorrow, but I am not sure until tomorrow comes. Then I suspect there will be the usual one on Memorial Day. Meanwhile, as I went down for the paper, I saw families in the old cemetery standing around and looking doubtful!

Anyway in Massachusetts there can never, never be a dull moment. Keeping up with the legislation is a full-time job. Two Memorial Days are really too many as far as I can see. Somehow it dilutes the significance—and I began to wonder whether two Christmases would come so as to make a long weekend around that holiday!

Most families survive one and that is enough.

There may be something more beautiful than an Irish setter running on a shining beach, but not to my way of thinking. Holly, my champion Irish, barely touched the sand with flying paws and her plumed tail blew like a sail. Mill Pond was her special place and when she had run enough, she plunged in the water and swam so far out I was always ner-

Finback whale stranded by the tide. (*John Schram*)

vous. All I could see was a dark mahogany wedge of nose.

There are, of course, a number of running breeds like greyhounds and Dalmatians and whippets, but the combination of grace and speed of the Irish is unequaled in the eyes of anyone owned by one. Retrievers and springers and English setters are of somewhat stockier build and tend to a slightly slower pace. Cockers will get through any kind of thicket and brush and never stop wagging, but they also are stockier in the shoulders.

Holly always came bounding up the steep steps from the beach fresh as a rosebud but dripping seaweed and salt. She had her own beach towel and after a rubdown sat patiently while we dealt with the tick problem. Ticks are the main reason to believe the Cape is not Paradise. They do not fly. They cling to tall grasses—or short ones—and fall off as people and dogs and kittens pass by. Then they burrow into the victim and gorge themselves with blood. They multiply rapidly so that sometimes you tweeze one out and already a host of barely visible offspring surround the spot.

I had never seen a tick until we came to Cape Cod, and we found them frightening. Occasional cases of Rocky Mountain spotted fever are carried by one type of tick but it is not endemic on the Cape. Nevertheless it was some time before I considered de-ticking just another routine.

Tick dips are satisfactory for dogs who do not swim but for water babies like Holly they are a waste of time. Handpicking twice or three times daily is the best remedy.

Everyone has a method. Mine is to twist the tick rapidly, then drop it in a jar of kerosene or Clorox. A friend of mine gets the ticks out and holds them to her cigarette lighter and never seems to burn her fingers off. Another friend uses tweezers and claims this way no head ever is left in to cause infection.

Tick and flea collars are favored by some and there are sprays too.

One story is that ticks were imported to the Cape along with a shipload of special rabbits. The dingy half-starved rabbits of today are loaded with them. Overpopulation has meant a food shortage and deficiency diseases, and also means nobody can grow as much as one rosebush without a San Quentin fence around it. I put in four or five very special roses one time and by the next morning they were stripped to the bone. Even the twigs were nibbled.

The natural balance should be maintained by foxes, but the encroachment of population has made foxes scarce. When my neighbors Millie and Ed see one fox, the whole neighborhood is in a glow. I have not seen it and I could really *walk* on rabbits at dusk in my yard.

This time of year, the Cape skunks wander around the road edges and often get killed trying to cross. There is no reason for a driver not to see a skunk in the road since they are big and striped with white. They cannot run fast but slowing down to let them reach the other side of the road is not much of a sacrifice!

My own skunk friend comes soberly across the lawn and goes down the steps to the beach. He prefers the steps to the grasses on either side and tiptoes from step to step like a careful banker on the way to the vault. I open the door and speak softly to him, and he turns and lifts his muzzle and peers at me with shiny eyes. He never raises his plumed weapon because he knows I mean well.

Last night Margaret Stanger came over shaking with excitement. The Scanlons' Irish setter was whelping and it was entirely unexpected. They had taken every precaution when she was in season and presumed she had had a false pregnancy.

My feeling was that a healthy, beautiful Irish with seven attendant neighboring males courting would somehow be able to find an open door when the milkman came or a package was delivered. And she had!

By the time we got there, four puppies were squealing and scrabbling under the dazed mother's chest. They were all in the bedroom beside the daughter's bed with emergency bedding around. Janeth Scanlon was worried because there was no whelping box. Her husband was off trying to get canned milk in case no milk was provided by the mother. Margaret and I went for baby nursing bottles in case supplementary feeding was necessary.

One rather special problem remained. Two visitors from Ghana were due this morning and the only double bedroom was full of puppies. Margaret offered her whole upstairs to the distinguished guests. I do not know anything about Ghana but I wondered if it might surprise the gentlemen to find a whole household revolving around a litter of unexpected, unpedigreed puppies!

By ten-thirty that night there were two black Labrador puppies and four Irish. Genetics is a mystery to me—why weren't the puppies just mixed in color and conformation? Red and black like Gordon setters? Or mostly black with red spottings? It did not worry the newborn at all. They simply wanted food after the hard work of being born.

They were still damp but the will to live was a miracle to watch, as always. They were about the size of soupspoons but pushed their tiny legs fiercely as they reached blindly for their mother.

As I sat watching the moon over Mill Pond, I felt comforted because in an era of preoccupation with death and new missiles for more death and new gases and poisons, still an Irish setter in an old Cape Cod house can repeat the greatest miracle on earth and produce new life instead of more death and be cherished for it.

The change toward summer is gentle on my mind, as the song goes. The wisteria on the Giles Hopkins place is now a cascade of amethyst, the biggest I have ever seen. I wonder which Hopkins planted it, for the wisteria over the old well house at Stillmeadow in Connecticut is well over thirty years old and is about a tenth of the size of this one. The long drooping clusters have an oriental look but the trunk stands solid in the Cape soil and looks as if it rightly belonged here.

The first wild rose has opened on the bushes outside my window. This rose is another signature of the Cape—a deep rosy almost-red, flat as a saucer, and with five big petals. The leaves are a shiny blue-green and the bushes grow all over the Cape in masses. Sandy, aerated soil, I am told, is what roses like best, and they seem to.

The tame or garden roses are poking out pointed buds, too, and I am apologizing as usual to the red rose which blooms earliest and latest and most profusely and which I never intended to have at all. It is a scraggly, unkempt bush no matter how it is trimmed, and the roses are in tight clusters and small blooms. They are a firehouse red, which is one color that does not fit anywhere in the house.

But they bloom and bloom and bloom, right up to and after frost. I have found I can make a small bouquet of them in a milk-glass mug and put them in the kitchen window where the background is the outdoors. And this morning when I went out with Amber, I noticed they will be blooming by next week.

The lilacs will be gone, the beach plum turned to rusty pink, the apple blossoms drifting in the lanes. Blankets blow on the lines and Snow's is jammed with women buying dust mops and garbage pails and bathmats and beach umbrellas.

June brings the tide of summer higher over the narrow land and the colors are as dramatic as Herb Alpert's trumpet. There is a sense of May orchestrating into June, which is both an excitement and a nostalgia—for do we ever have enough of May?

A petal moon is shining as I say goodnight to springtime —tomorrow will not be exactly the same!

Summer

SONNET FOR SKAKET

We shall be gone tomorrow from this place
Where now we watch the westering sun descend
Into her wide and quiet sea where space
Has neither a beginning nor an end.
We shall not see the last reluctant tide
Leaving the pools of pearl, or sanderlings,
Or twilight terns that circle as they ride
Cresting the wave of air that day's end brings.

The sun goes down, taking the light with her,
While two late swimmers make their way
From the far deep where silver ripples stir.
Nothing is left, dear love, of this bright day.
And yet this hour of joy we shall remember
Comes the inevitable, comes November.

Now I know summer is here, no matter how cold it is at night, for when I went out to the car this morning, the windshield was dusted with orange and the whole shiny dark blue of the body was powdered. The pine pollen has come! This is a thick, almost oily, deposit that penetrates everything. If you close a room and lock the windows, the sills will be drifted with the pollen the next morning. The floors turn orange.

Painting and cleaning chores must be postponed. And no use airing things on the line. I decided to organize the bookshelves in the wing and found pollen behind those volumes that had not been moved all winter.

It is a bad time for asthma sufferers. I used to dread it especially for Bobby Gibson, then a thin, leggy boy in his subteens. When he turned up on a lovely night to play folksongs on the stereo and brought, as usual, nice hot pizzas from Packet Landing, but came in gasping and half-bent over, I knew the pollen season had begun.

"Off to the doctor in the morning," I said.

Then I would hook up the room air-conditioner for Jill, my housemate of many years. Her wheezing was deeper than Bobby's and with more coughing. But Jill was never one for coddling.

"You can take that thing out," she would choke. "I am not going to be shut up in a tomb with that motor."

"You could have it on at night," I suggested.

"I want the windows open. I need fresh air!"

Last June I found the air-conditioner in the closet in her bedroom. It had been a fancy one, you fed it *ice cubes!* On a hot breathless night it could gulp all the ice in the freezer in half an hour or so. I turned it on and a long oily sigh resulted. Ginny Cook, my neighbor, dropped in at that moment to see if I had anything to go to the dump (I always have) and after a quick examination, she said she would take the air-conditioner, too, to the dump as she went.

This led me to my favorite musing about future generations excavating the Orleans dump and analyzing our civilization from the remains. I often sit at the dump just looking and thinking about the discards from smashed automobiles (which do not belong there) to old wicker lawn chairs, from broken radios to bound volumes of stock reports from 1952. But the greatest tide is always rags—bits of old clothing, rat-chewed rugs, torn drapes.

I have friends who find priceless antiques at the dump which they do over, old sea chests, early pine mirror-frames, sewing tables. But I pick my way through very dead lobster shells and quahogs. I never glean so much as a piece of driftwood for the fireplace.

The bridal wreath is at its peak this week—early in June. The cemetery is bordered with cascades of white and a good many dooryards are banked with it. I wonder whether I would love it if I had never seen it until I came across the bridge? It depresses me and I cannot reason myself out of it. The association must be there—for life is nothing much but building associations.

It takes me back to the middle west where I grew up (after my father settled down to be a professor instead of a mining engineer). I was passionately happy there in a house we belonged to and with school friends and with the trunks and suitcases put away in the attic. But there was something about the bridal wreath, which grew lavishly all over the small river town, especially around the Catholic and Protestant cemeteries and also, I think, around the hospital grounds. When there were funerals, as there were rather often, bridal wreath made lovely bouquets if the funeral was in June.

In any case, it depresses me and as I drive past the really elegant hedges of it, I turn my head and look instead at the white lilacs on the other side. The purple are gone but the white still lift delicate snowy spears.

One special memory of mine is the year Jill and I were invited to be guests on one of the fishing boats during the ceremony of the Blessing of the Fleet. Provincetown was not so crowded then, nor invaded by the curly-haired unwashed young. It was a Portuguese fishing village originally and fishing was still a major industry.

The boats were decorated with pennants and lined up at the pier rocking gently in the swell. The procession from the church, led by the priests, came down the steep hill and there was the ceremony of the Blessing, which was very moving.

Then everyone was on board and the boats cast off, heading out into the sapphire water. The captain of our boat was a handsome young Portuguese and one of the town officers. He was everything one would expect of a captain. Plus glamorous.

I think it was his wife who wore the elegant straw hat with flowers all around the brim, lifting gay blue and pink and green cups.

As we cruised farther out, the food began to appear, along with kegs of foamy rich beer and Portuguese wines. Never has food been so delicious, not in Paris, not in an exclusive New York restaurant. Big chunky sandwiches of Portuguese bread were served (the very best there is) with spiced meats and cheeses.

It was clouding up, but we did not notice. The captain did seem to be jumping around some but the singing went on. Then when the storm hit, like an upside-down volcano in its fury, the sturdy fishing boat heeled over. Water gushed across the deck. Lightning split the sky.

The little flower cups on that hat filled with water and it poured down the wearer's hapless neck. Everyone was clinging to something. Except, I must admit, me.

I crawled across the swimming deck with something in a napkin.

"What in the world are you doing?" wheezed Jill.

"If I'm going to drown," I said, "I'm going to have more of those sausage things first."

I was not really courageous. I think I had a firm subconscious belief that no boat could sink with that captain in charge. It didn't either, although this was a rather severe flash storm and some of the boats had a bad time getting back.

When we finally got back to the pier, I had only one bite left of that memorable rain-soaked delicacy.

As life becomes more pedestrian and regimented, I am sorry that so often we give up the color and charm of traditional ceremonies such as this. I am sentimental, I know, by today's bitter standards, but I like America the Beautiful even though it won't be that much longer. I like candle-lighting ceremonies. I like May baskets with their implication of friendship and love when flowers bloom. And the Blessing of the Fleet was an experience I shall treasure always.

One special feature of June on Cape Cod is that every other car pulls a boat behind it. It is not easy to turn a sharp corner with a trailer and a whale-size craft swaying along on it. It is often hard to see over the prow of the boat and driv-

Crystal Lake in Orleans, one of more than 300 freshwater
ponds on Cape Cod. (*John Schram*)

ers peer earnestly in their side mirrors (a feat I have never mastered).

Nothing looks more helpless and awkward than a boat out of the water being hauled along like a freight car. Then when this same bulky craft is lowered into the water a miracle takes place. Light and graceful as a swan, the prow meets the ripples. But I notice, with the realistic side of me, that half the time after the boats are launched, the motors will not run. I stop working to look out at Mill Pond and see desperate mariners hauling away at the motors and finally trying to move along with one oar. My final opinion is that motor-boating is hard work and I prefer canoeing, which is the transportation we always used. The paddles always worked!

Now a sailboat is romance in motion. My favorite is the Sailfish, which is merely a shell with one sail over it. Right now Robin Lovely and Holly Morrison are tacking across Mill Pond. The sail is triangular and bigger than the boat and is striped with dark blue which echoes the blue of the water. The boat herself is so flat that from my window it looks as if the two teenagers were floating in the sea itself.

They spend a whole afternoon, just slowly skimming back and forth and exchanging those profound thoughts which teenagers must share with one another. It is so still that even the cry of the gulls has ceased. I think how fortunate these Cape youngsters are to have the gift of quiet in their lives. On Mill Pond there is no juke box, no hippie band, no screaming of obscenities. Robin and Holly are enjoying a heritage I wish all teenagers could share.

I remember well the age at which a girl must have a best friend. It precedes and overlaps the first suffocating love for the first boy. I think it provides a small armor against that cataclysm, although I do not remember any experts saying so.

Mine was a tall, gangly pencil of a girl named Peggy who lived way across town—perhaps three miles away. We had no Sailfish and she did not have a bicycle. But it was a shadowy kind of dream town we lived in, set in the green Wisconsin hills. We could walk along tree-canopied streets and talk and talk and talk. First she walked me home and then I walked her home and then she walked me back halfway and then I walked her back halfway.

I would be late for supper and my father in a rage, but my mother did her best to calm him down. "Rufus," she would say in her soft voice, "they have their schoolwork to talk about."

It is strange what evokes memories—Cape Cod and Mill Pond are halfway across the country and half a lifetime away from that little river town, but when I see Robin and Holly in the blue Sailfish, I am suddenly back under the elms, smelling the sulphur smell of the air in that town (which I loved) and hearing Peggy's languid voice say "I don't know—but if everybody who EVER died is still alive somewhere, won't it get kind of crowded?"

On the way to Rock Harbor last night I saw the yellow tea roses in bloom on Main Street and memory again turned time back. The old-fashioned bush rose which blossoms early in June and bears clusters of small, creamy-yellow blooms is rare in these parts and also in my Connecticut valley. It has a Victorian aura some way, suggesting tea in silver teapots served in arbored garden closes. One thinks of ladies in full skirts and satin slippers.

Someone will correct me and say this is not a tea rose, just a bush rose, but a tea rose was what it was called in my childhood and it did bloom just when days were balmy enough for tea to be served out-of-doors.

I noticed the dark purple iris has come out all along the way, just overnight. Sometimes I wonder whether, if one stayed awake day and night and sat right by a plant or bush, one would ever SEE the unfolding of a petal! I am sure experts have set fancy cameras to monitor growth, but the human eye is not so mechanical. Yesterday the iris held stiff, varnished buds up. Today the velvety chalices are open.

The honey locusts are a Cape specialty and the air tastes like wine when they bloom. The bees make honey from them with a flavor that cannot be copied.

The phone rang this noon and Helen Beals said, "I just wanted to call you and say the bees are back. They are swarming under the eaves so if you come over, be very careful."

She went on to say her son had stopped up every hole but somehow they were there and had gotten into the attic and were swarming all over the place.

"And I wonder if the weight of the honey will break the ceiling down in the front bedroom!" she said.

"I don't think it would be that heavy," I told her, knowing *nothing* about the weight of honey from swarms of bees.

"We once had a man come to lure them away," she went on. "A man who had bees. It didn't make any difference to them. They just come back here."

"I bet they are descendants of bees who were here in 1812," I commented. "You know how scarce sugar was then —maybe someone tried to keep bees at the Inn to get honey for hot buttered rum."

"Well," said Helen, "I don't need them in my attic!"

"I'll be over tomorrow," I told her. "Nothing ever stings me and it does make me wonder sometimes what is wrong —there are all kinds of unhappy thoughts that go with this, especially if you watch TV commercials. But my daughter, Connie, and my granddaughters, at ten and eight, can swell up in five minutes if they just walk past a mosquito or stinging insect."

Poison ivy never affected me, either, until I sat down in a

bed of it one twilight while fishing. Since then I do not pull it up by the roots if it gets in the garden. The sandy Cape soil is very hospitable to poison ivy and whole banks of it lift glossy elegant leaves and bear the scarlet berries which the birds can eat without after-effects. One autumn, a friend brought me a lovely bouquet of branches with frosty silvery clusters of berries. I had never seen anything like them and neither had she. She spent a session in the hospital before long with a deadly case of poison ivy. I was fine. But I had not waded in the thickets to pick these late treasures. I just put them in an antique bottle and enjoyed them!

It was early in the morning when I went to the veterinarian's today. It was also Saturday and a fine gold-and-blue June day, and I remarked morosely to Amber that she could have waited until a Monday to have her lip swell up. I knew better, for years and years of raising cockers and Irish and owning cats has taught me that when they are going to have anything wrong, it has to be on a weekend, preferably Sunday when the veterinarian's office is closed.

The traffic toward Provincetown was boiling along, so I had to pray as I turned left for Dr. Kim's hospital. Formerly my Catholic friends protected me with a medal of St. Christopher, but today I realized he was no longer available. His church had given him up.

The office was already jammed but I found one seat in a corner and put Amber's carrying case beside the table. During the next hour or more I had time to study Cape Cod in a special way. There were four dogs who had been run over. They were all hit in the hind legs—they could not run fast enough to escape the speeding cars. All but one could still walk, with a shambling stagger. Kim had to carry one Labrador into the treatment room.

There was a Brittany spaniel with some unidentified ail-

ment and there was a mixed-breed, blanketed with ticks.
There were several cats.

As they came out of the inner room with splints and band-
ages, I watched the owners and thought about them. There
were the summer residents, older ones, with neatly waved
hair and cool vacation-print frocks and wearing stockings
and flat shoes. More and more of the year these people are
also Cape Cod.

Then there were two young mothers in jeans and sweatshirts. Small, scrubbed boys belonged to them and when the
mothers spoke, the Cape accent labeled them.

"Is your dog a golden retriever?" one was asked.

"Pahtly," she said, "only pahtly."

Two lean-hipped, middle-aged men came in. They had the
weathered look of fishermen. The true fishermen I have observed all have lines around their eyes from squinting and this
gives them the look of being about to smile. The eyes themselves are usually narrowed but very bright. The mouths are
compressed as if they didn't talk much when the dories are
pitching and heaving far from shore.

They have a look of security which is hard to pin down
and they speak with deliberation. One of these had tattoos
over one bare arm but I could not decipher them because a
small anxious puppy was cradled in that arm and the owner's
big square left hand was gentled on the small muzzle.

The two hippies who came were not together, but they
leaned against the wall as close to each other as possible as if
seeking protection. They were in the early twenties and
wore the usual fur on head and face, thick dark fur which reminded me that man was an arboreal creature once (as I always am reminded when I see these youngsters). One wore
faded jeans with insets of a flowered cretonne on the pant-
legs. The other had stained corduroys on. Both wore sandals
with single thongs.

One of them just told the nurse, "I want to see the doctor. I want to see the doctor." His small black mongrel was lively and clean-looking but I heard him telling the second hippie in a low tone that she had ticks, just lots of ticks.

"I've got to get a dip for her," he said.

He might be willing to go unwashed and uncombed himself but his dog was not to have the same treatment!

The door opened at this point to admit a man big enough to carry the ceiling on his shoulders. He had no dog or cat but went to the window and pulled out a wallet. He wore high-heeled, decorated, well-worn boots, Western-style pants and shirt and one of those broad-brimmed hats which they always wear tilted to one side, and which never really fit the head size but perch as migratory birds do on treetops in fall. He mopped his face with a very blue bandanna, paid his bill and clicked out.

Finally, just before it was my turn, two more men came in with a closed carton big enough to house a stereo. It was awkward to carry and they set it on the desk with some difficulty. What they had inside was a cat, for they came over to admire Amber's carrying case and to ask what kind of cat she is.

"That's quite a case. She can see out," they both said. Their carton had two small breathing holes but was sealed with package tape at the top.

At this point a bouncy Manchester terrier dragged his mistress in.

"What is that strange noise?" asked one of the young mothers nervously.

"Well, it is my cat," I said.

The whole waiting room concentrated on my cat—the smallest person there, only the size of one paw of most of the patients. But I could hardly fail to admit where the noise was coming from, since the whole carrying case vibrated with it.

I had to bend over to be sure, for Amber had never created such a sound in her life before. It sounded like those old-time warning bells that kept mariners from hidden reefs in the days of sailing ships. I have no idea how her small fragile self could produce this tolling vibrance.

All the dogs wanted to come right over, and the cat in the carton began to lunge around inside. The ebony cat with the elegant harness and effete manners widened emerald eyes and quivered too.

"She's just getting a little nervous," I said apologetically.

But Amber wasn't nervous. She was furious. Her seal-brown tail was lashing and whenever she stopped the tolling, she paused long enough to hiss. She was fed up with sitting in that waiting room in that carrying case and with people poking their noses in her air holes as they went by and the last curious puppy that stared through the plastic top was simply too much.

"All right, bring Amberino in," said Kim. "You're next."

Five minutes later we were on the way home with Amber's lip swabbed with disinfectant. One of the men in the waiting room picked up her case and went to the car with it and put her in the front seat.

This also was typical of Cape Cod, I thought. Generalizations are never true but if one could be, it would be that many people on the Cape take time to be kind because there is less pressure than in inland, urban areas. This helpful man was, I noted, not a native. He was a city businessman come for a hurried weekend. But he reflected the Cape nevertheless.

When we got back, Amber ate a second breakfast while I had more coffee and thought about the veterinarians who give their lives to help suffering animals. They seldom have any time off, for when the office is not full, the patients in the hospital need constant care. What's more, they have to treat not only the patients but the owners, so they have a double job and the owners are more trouble than the patients as a rule.

The veterinarians I have been devoted to all have an optimistic temperament, however. And they usually feel like Dr. Bernstein who, after a miraculous rescue operation, simply remarked, "We don't make mistakes."

Kim's optimism includes his faith in me, which is sometimes misplaced.

"Just put a cold compress on that lip," he said this morning.

I did not point out that when he put medicine on it he had his assistant and me and both of his own deft hands to help. Three of us kept my five-pound Aby on the table.

How he could lightly assume that all by myself I could apply a cold compress to that petal mouth was surprising. A sixty-five-pound Irish setter is no problem, but a kitten is just different!

Pret Barker brought me a mess of steamers from Mill Pond this morning. His wire basket was full of the small, smoke-blue clams still dripping with sea water.

"I got them all under water," he said, "so they'll be sweeter."

The shells are almost transparent and break easily. The clam itself is the most delicate of the shellfish so that inexpert diggers often crush the shells and destroy the steamer.

I scrubbed them under cold running water, then put them in a pan with a few tablespoons of clean water and a dollop of butter. I covered the pan and steamed them until the shells opened. This was about four minutes—bigger and older clams might take a bit more. The broth went in a mug and an egg cup of melted butter accompanied the bowl of clams.

Then I had a feast!

Quahogs are bigger and with heavier shells. Some people use clam rakes to dig them but I prefer the hand method. There are tiny spout holes which show where the quahogs are, and you simply bend down and scoop the treasures out of the mud. Quahogs are the chowder clams and also are gourmet eating when stuffed and baked.

The beach below Still Cove has plenty of both steamers and quahogs and a little farther toward Duck Pond, there are mussels, lovely rich purple clusters clinging to the rocks just under water.

Many people do not realize how delicious they are, so they are more readily available.

DEVILED CLAMS

1 dozen large hard-shelled clams or quahogs
6 tbsp. prepared seasoned stuffing
2 tbsp. light cream
3 tbsp. chopped parsley
1 tbsp. chopped green pepper
1 tsp. Worcestershire sauce
1 tbsp. butter or margarine
1 drop Tabasco
Seasoned pepper or freshly ground to taste.

Scrub clams and put in a flat baking pan in a hot oven (450°) until the shells open. Save the clam juice. Finely mince the clams, then add 2 tbsp. of the juice, half the stuffing and the rest of the ingredients.

When the juice is absorbed, spoon mixture into clam shells, top with the rest of the stuffing and dot with butter. Lay the stuffed clams on a baking sheet and bake in a moderate oven (350°) until browned. This takes 15 minutes, about. Do not overcook as the clams will be tough.

Serves 6 as a first course or luncheon dish—or is elegant with cocktails.

Quahogging in Salt Pond, Eastham. (*John Schram*)

If I do not have fresh clams, I often make the baked stuffed clams with canned minced clams. This is something to keep secret from Cape Cod diggers! For one 7½-oz.-can minced clams, drained, you need 2 tbsp. melted butter, ¼ cup seasoned bread crumbs, ⅓ cup clam juice, ½ tsp. lemon juice (I use a bit more), ½ tsp. seasoned salt, ¼ tsp. basil, ¼ tsp. marjoram, ¼ tsp. thyme, a few drops Worcestershire sauce. Mix all ingredients well. Spread in clam shells, dot with butter, grated cheese and paprika. Bake in oven (350°) for 20 minutes. Let cool slightly and serve. Serves 6.

Now for the Steamed Mussels I use a dozen mussels, which must be scrubbed well and rinsed. Melt 2 tbsp. butter in a large pot or Dutch oven and add ½ cup chopped shallots and a garlic clove. Cook until slightly brown, then remove garlic. Stir in 2 tbsp. flour and blend until smooth. When bubbles form around the edge, remove from heat and slowly stir in 1 cup good white wine, some chopped parsley, ¼ tsp. salt, ¼ tsp. dried basil, dash of freshly ground pepper. Simmer 5 minutes, then add mussels and cover. Simmer 5 more minutes, stirring occasionally until shells open. Serve in heated bowls with crusty French bread chunks for dunking in the sauce.

I used to eat in New York City with my publisher at a French restaurant where Moules Marinières were the main feature. They served the mussels in silver bowls and the hot bread in woven baskets and there was imported white wine to go with the menu.

Now on Cape Cod, I serve the mussels in antique onion-pattern soup bowls.

Cape Cod Clam Chowder is the only true clam chowder, to my way of thinking. A lot of potato soup passes itself off as chowder and the Manhattan Clam Chowder is just a tomato and clam soup. For the real dish, you take 2 dozen hard-shelled clams in the shell and scrub them well. Put in a deep kettle and pour over 1 cup of water. Steam, tightly covered, until shells open. Remove clams and chop hard portions with a sharp knife. Strain juice through cheesecloth and add 2 cups water. Meanwhile, dice ¼ lb. salt pork and heat over low heat until crisp and golden brown. Add 1 minced onion and when the onion is transparent, add hard portions of the clams. Cook slowly 5 minutes. Sprinkle 3 tbsp. flour over and add clam juice and water. Add 2 cups raw sliced or diced potatoes, cover, and cook until potatoes are tender. Then add soft part of clams and 3 tbsp. butter and when this comes to a boil, add 4 cups heated (not boiling) milk. Add paprika, parsley, salt, pinch of thyme. Let the chowder ripen at least half an hour. Then reheat until piping hot and serve in heated soup bowls with toasted chowder crackers. If you are not dieting you may use part light cream and part milk (delicious). This is said to serve 6 but try it on 3!

If we are lucky enough to have fresh oysters from Wellfleet, we usually want to eat them right out of the shell, but Scalloped Oysters are fine for a cold foggy night. For 4 people you need 1 pint drained oysters (save the liquor). In a shallow greased baking pan put a layer of ½ cup bread crumbs, 1 cup cracker crumbs, ½ cup melted butter, mixed together well. Lay the oysters gently on this bed and cover with the rest of the crumbs. Pour the oyster liquor and 1 tbsp. cream over. Season with salt and freshly ground pepper and bake in a hot oven (450°) for 20 minutes or so. A dusting of paprika does no harm as you take the savory pan from the oven.

For a party of 8, oyster stew is a fine extravagance. You use 3 dozen oysters shucked and with the liquid. Heat 5 tbsp. butter in a heavy kettle and when it bubbles, add the oysters and seasonings—2 tbsp. Worcestershire (what would we do without it?), 1 tsp. seasoned salt, ½ tsp. freshly ground pepper, ½ cup minced parsley (or more if you like), 1 tsp. paprika. When the edge of the oysters begins to curl (about 1 minute) add the heated milk—6 cups top milk or half milk and half cream. Simmer briefly but never let it boil. Let stand to blend the flavors while the guests have their favorite cocktails. When ready to serve, heat the stew again but watch it —it must not boil. Pour into a warm tureen and dust with more paprika and parsley.

Perhaps the only cardinal rule with clams, mussels, oysters (or lobsters and shrimp for that matter) is *never overcook*. Most seafood gets rubbery and tough and loses its delicate flavor if it is cooked too long.

I do love fried clams but I prefer to get them from Philbrick's at Nauset because they are better than any I could do, and it is fun to eat them in the car while the surf thunders in and the seagulls ride the air.

The honey locust is a tree, I think, but on my land it is a shrub in shape, stocky and low. When it blooms, as it is doing now, the long slender pointed leaves are barely visible, for the creamy spikes of small florets give the effect of a snowdrift. Few trees blossom so passionately.

The fragrance is thick and sweet. I feel you could slice it with a silver knife and spread it on freshly baked bread. The bees know what to do with the treasure they gather and as they zoom around they are dusted with pollen. It is a pity bees cannot know of their invaluable contribution to mankind in the pollination of so many species dependent on them for reproduction.

Along Tonset there are bigger locusts, partly because that is the cove side of the Cape and more protected. Somehow they remind me of the fountains of Rome as the white lilacs do.

The iris grows tall on the narrow land and spreads a tapestry of color. The black-purple is naturally my favorite but there is a chestnut brown and beige that is spectacular and one with amethyst and white petals. And dozens of other variations. My neighbors went away for a couple of weeks and I cut their iris two days ago. It is not an easy flower to arrange without having a stiff bouquet, but I used a soft green rectangular pottery jar and made a plain triangle and felt I had succeeded.

With this type of flower, the problem of adding greenery is acute. The iris I cut looked like small telephone poles with a flag on the tips. But you cannot fill in with trailing vines like honeysuckle. Iris is too rigid. I settled for tips of a piney shrub whose name I do not even know.

The iris will soon be gone and the June roses will take over. Already there is one lonely Rugosa opening on the bank back of the house.

Perhaps if I were to give advice to anyone wanting to move to the Cape, it would be simple. "Don't come unless you can mow your lawn and do your own gardening." I can't do either, so I sit and watch the honeysuckle smother the roses and pines and lilacs and the poison ivy come in between the steps to the beach.

I did achieve a triumph last week with the help of Robin Lovely, who came over to help with a few chores and I said I had two bags of loam (loom here) and eighteen petunia plants and those two windowboxes full of weeds.

The story of the windowboxes is odd because they just sit flat *on* the ground and Ted O'Gorman made them for me so I could have a few flowers by the front door. Holly had dug up anything that went in the ground by the front door as fast as she could paw, making deep excavations to lie in on warm days. So big wooden boxes were set in above ground and she could not lie in them.

This was the only time in our lives I crossed her, and the windowboxes did upset her. But it had been embarrassing for guests to pick their way through a mess of dying petunias, geraniums or whatever to get to the door, and they always brought a lot of loom in with them.

Robin did a fine job and then said she hoped the petunias would live. All the planting she had ever done before was to help Daddy put in the peas! As of today, the eighteen are all in fine health and I water the boxes heavily.

And if anyone thinks this is easy, that is another error. There is not a faucet at Still Cove high enough to put a watering-can nose under, not even the bathtub. The outside, nonrust, waterproof, freeze-proof, etc., faucets not only are about an inch from the ground, but once turned on, can only be turned off by a strong man. So the hoses sleep like coiled snakes in the cellar.

I brought the watering-can in the kitchen and set it on the table. Then I filled it with the help of an antique pitcher which will *just* go under the faucet. Seven pitchers later, I had the watering-can full.

Then there was a minor problem, since it seemed to drip; but I got it out of the front door finally and I watered those petunias!

By then I had done my gardening for the day but I still had the geranium tubs to do by the wing door. Even if it rains, they seldom get a drop of water. Rain seems to go right by them. I had had enough of the watering-can, so I filled a shallow plastic wash basin with water and opened the wing door and flung the water out. Two rounds made the tubs look like a high tide and I hoped they were satisfied.

I comfort myself by thinking most people who come here are dazzled by the view, which at least is not my responsibility. Nature herself takes care of it. And what I should do is never look at the ground around the house but look past the weeds and smothering shrubs and simply enjoy the expanse of blue-green water and the serenity of a clear sky.

When I went to the DeLorys' last night I was surprised to find a load of hay in their yard. They live in the deep woods by the water and have no livestock at all. But there were all these bales of hay. So Jimmy explained this is called the lazy man's garden on the Cape. Eileen had gone to Taylor's farm and bought spoiled hay. I do not know what spoils it but that is what they call it. You spread this spoiled hay on a place where you want to plant a garden. After a year or so, you plant in it and you never have to weed.

I had seen a similar pile of hay at Slim Lovely's shortly before, but since I knew Barbara is a horse fanatic and Robin might also want a horse, I assumed this was the first step toward a stable. I now knew Slim also was making a new garden out of spoiled hay!

I shall watch with great interest the progress of these mysterious weedless gardens!

Another Cape specialty is lawns made of pine chips instead of grass. The chips are spread all over the yard so whatever grows there seems to be poking its head through a turtleneck collar. This obviously never has to be mowed or weeded or watered. For tucking around foundation planting, as it is at Dr. Dickson's, the effect is fine, but a slope of it leading to a house looks like a glacial moraine. The color is a grayish brown. A variation of this is pine needles, which look better.

There have been times when I wondered whether the pine needles might be my fate. But so far someone always turns up to mow just before the weeds are knee-high.

Driveways here are usually hard-topped although some householders are fortunate enough to have shell driveways. We began with one, by putting all of our quahog and steamer shells in heaps in the drive and then running over them. We soon found out that raw shells attract every kind of insect as well as wandering seagulls. Our shell road buzzed with activity. It also smelled. But the pearl and gray-colored

shells are lovely to look at, and if you survive until the shells
have been there long enough, you have a handsome driveway. A sand driveway is common and the owner of such
says, "Watch for the holes. Some bad ones in the middle.
Washed out."

Sand will fall into deep ruts at the turn of one truck wheel
and these fill with water at every rainfall. A kind of soup re-
sults.

I resisted the hard top on Blue Rock Road because I felt,
quite rightly, that it would persuade people to drive down
out of curiosity, whereas if it were a single track in the sand
they might not. There is no road past Still Cove and the
woods are too thick for even a drunken driver to attack. So
whoever comes down the road ends outside my windows—
and I found it very comfortable to know when I heard the
sound of automobile brakes, someone was coming to see me.

But the sand road gave out when the Barkers next door
built their wing, and my own driveway was too full of extra
ridges which I tried to level off by jumping up and down on
them. This is not a permanent road-repair job!

Now we are used to the hard-top road and we have kept it
only one car-width wide as a suggestion it is not a through-
way. The sign says PRIVATE ROAD, but most Cape road signs
say that. Nobody reads them.

But on Champlain Road and the end of Mill Pond, the
town has been patching chuckholes with something that
looks like tar but smells like rotten fish. At first I tried holding my breath as I drove there, but the distance is too long
and I ended collapsing with vertigo over the wheel. I tried
muffling my face with Kleenex but that did not work either.

Finally I had a really intelligent idea. I ran all the car windows up tight before I got near the repair area and then
drove safely past while breathing nothing but carbon monox-
ide or whatever it is. I hope to find out whether they grind

up dead fish and stir them in this road material or somehow get fish oil. It is strong stuff, for a good deal of rain has fallen on that stretch of road and over a month has passed. And it still smells.

Mid-June theoretically begins summer on the 21st at 8:55 A.M. Trees are in full leaf and the leaves will not grow any more. This means a change in the cycle as they turn toward the storing of their resources against the winter to come. The leaves are glossy and polished because the heat of August is still some time away and June brings plenty of rain on the Cape as a rule. Nights are cool, too, down around 45 to 50 and the misty fingers of fog reach in often at dusk.

If you cup your hand, you can feel the fog even when you cannot see the droplets. It is clammy and cool.

I do not like to drive in it, but Cape Codders pay no more attention to it than we do inland to driving in a blizzard. But when it is not possible to see either side of the road, I do not feel at ease. A few times when I have been out in a night fog with Margaret Stanger, she has had to walk along the edge of the road to direct me while I crunched slowly after her.

I get lots of advice. Use only low-beam lights. Just look at one side of the road, not both at once. Get out now and then and find the middle of the road. My own advice is easier: *stay home* if I can't see my own beach from the front terrace!

The Full Hot Moon comes the 28th this month and it is time for strawberry shortcake and moonlight picnics and for swimming. Hardy souls have been venturing in the ocean briefly before, but 40 degrees is not an easy water temperature, especially with a brisk sea breeze blowing. From now on, the swimming will be wonderful. The sunburning will also begin and the town will be full of roasted humanity as man reverts to a worship of the sun god, which began in pre-

historic times and is still with us. The sun is, after all, the
source of heat and light, and a sunless world would not last
long.

The Cape Cod telephone book will always be a mystery to
me. I have studied it faithfully and feel it is my own limita-
tion that I can't solve the problem of making a phone call
off-Cape—or even on.

For Hyannis, it is 1 plus 7 numerals. For Orleans, it is 7 numerals. For Naushon Island, it is Operator. Names are not
listed by towns but by the alphabet, so unless you have an
idea where people live you may call Nickersons, Eldredges,
Snows, Webbs and so on all day long. There is a half page of
Mayos. There is also one other Taber, who is a Tabor and
runs a fishing boat, so that I am often waked up by calls at
seven in the morning when someone wants to reach Captain
Tabor.

Calling off-Cape is even more difficult for me than reaching the Connors. Today I decided to call my publisher's office in New York and discuss something with Tay Hohoff,
the editor there. First I studied the map with its tiny figures
and found 212 for New York City, tucked in behind three
other zone numbers for New York. Then I read the book
and learned I should dial 1 to call Boston, then the telephone
number but NOT the area code. For Providence, Rhode Island, I should dial 1, then area code, then telephone number.

I found on page 7 that 212 was right for Brooklyn and
New York City. So I found Lippincott's number in my address book, Murray Hill and 5 digits. By this time I was
sweating. But I dialed everything, and like a miracle got an
answer.

What I got was an insurance company in New York City
with a number not remotely resembling the one I had dialed.
We had a nice conversation, the agent and I, and I apolo-

gized. So I decided on a person-to-person call and began on
that. Operator told me firmly to get the off-Cape line—
110. After ten minutes the off-Cape line roused itself to answer. What ensued was fictional.

"You want to call long distance New York City?" she
couldn't believe it.

"Please, a person-to-person call to T A Y H O H O F F
at—"

"Are you *SPELLING* a name for me?"

"Well, I was. I thought you might like to know whom I
am trying to call."

"All right, spell it."

I spelled it. She could not believe there was such a name.
Finally convinced, she was willing to struggle with J. B. Lippincott and Fifth Avenue, and then asked me if I was still on
the wire.

I admitted I was. Ensued a long colloquy between this girl
and another operator, presumably farther inland. Party wants
to call New York City. J. B. Lippincott—How do you
spell that? Please spell it again. Does it begin with L? L I P?
Repeat the name of the party.

Ten minutes later, I heard a ring and a familiar and comforting voice say, "J. B. Lippincott."

"Long distance call for Mr. Tay Hohoff," said my operator. "Wait until I find out the name." Then to me, "Who's
calling?"

"Gladys Taber," I murmured faintly.

Tay, who is a lovely woman, could not see why I was
breathless at reaching her. She was right there in the office
the whole time!

I realize the phone service is part of the new computerized
living and we cannot go back to the days when Central could
say exactly where Mrs. Russell had gone and when she would
be back. You could discuss things with the operator then and

also get bits of news. An answering service you cannot even talk back to.

I mention this kind of thing every now and then as a part of the nervous strain of present-day living. When I was a child, I had one number to remember—7—our house was 7 Brokaw Place. Now, in nightmares, I find I have lost my social security number, my zip code, my bank identification, my car license number, and the ten digits that should go on the bottom of every dividend check. In a few years, children will be named Four and Five, like Beverly Nichols' cats. I can see it coming, even on Cape Cod!

On the way to Rock Harbor, I noticed today the weigela bushes are so heavy with bloom that the branches are almost flat on the ground. This is a bush that has a tropical exuberance with the deep pink blossoms set so close that no green is visible until the end of the bloom time. The individual florets are shaped rather like trumpet flowers and they pour out along the stems. As they fade, they have a bluish or rusty pink tinge and well, I admit, they look tarnished.

In the house, in a bouquet, the blossoms begin to fall almost at once so I rarely struggle with them, handsome as they are. For some reason I had never seen this bush until I came to the Cape and it is associated with June going by always too fast and with the imminence of July. But my two bushes by the wing have had no care at all and they cascade rosy splendor all over the slope. They do not get fed or sprayed or dug around, they simply grow and bloom.

In an odd way, they are an inspiration to me. They survive on their own. They bloom. They ask no odds of anybody. I think this is a quality we need more of in the present day. I would be glad if I could climb up the bank and prune them and fertilize them and tend to them. But they bourgeon on their own!

This Wednesday I went to a cocktail party on Mayflower Point. I went to meet a golden retriever eight-week-old puppy imported from Canada who had just arrived. I expected to find the puppy and his new parents and Jimmy and Eileen DeLory, but there were at least fifty guests there. I find large groups too difficult because of the noise and seldom get involved in anything that counts up to more than six or eight.

But the hostess brought this solid lump of golden puppy out and plumped him in my arms at once.

He stood the noise better than I did, and kept washing my face earnestly as we visited and I have to report this as the most successful cocktail party I have been to for a long time.

He has the blocky muzzle of the golden, which is not like the nose of an Irish, but the sweet outgoing temperament is the same. The eyes are more three-cornered and not so large, and the ears, at this age, mere triangles like sailfish sails.

I noted he had digits tattooed on the inner side of one ear, which means he also belongs in this age of numbers. I suppose if he got lost, the tattoo might help, but the old-fashioned metal tag with the license number and address and "Precious Lamb" also worked very well.

The tattoo idea would help in wholesale stealing of dogs, however, as a tag and collar can always be dumped in the nearest trash container but a tattoo is a permanent fixture.

The next day I went to the christening of the half-Irish and half-Labrador litter at the Scanlons', now just opening milky blue eyes. All eight are fine, chirping away with those bird noises the very young puppies have, yawning a lot, and nuzzling for food.

The Scanlons' young daughter, Judy, came out carrying the black-and-white cat.

"Mrs. Taber," she said shyly, "can you tell me how soon she will have her kittens?"

"You mean kittens *and* all those puppies. What *will* you do?"

Janeth Scanlon, her mother, has a serene face and simply smiled. "We'll fix another carton for the kittens," she said.

June is really over although nights are cool. Robin Lovely and Holly Morrison stayed in swimming most of the afternoon today, mostly just floating around, which means the water is no longer paralyzing but reasonably comfortable.

So I really think it is time to get the screen doors on before the fourth of July!

But two finalities impressed me this Monday afternoon when I went over to the Lovelys'. Richard Lovely was back from Ohio Wesleyan, having graduated the past weekend, and was perched at the kitchen table eating a pint of chocolate ice cream and a quarter of a chocolate layer cake.

"After all," he said, "I had lunch half an hour ago!"

Then I saw the kitchen floor was like the hold of a ship with thirty or thirty-five enormous shopping bags spilling over their contents, everything from paper plates and cups to detergents and canned goods.

"Now what's happened?" I asked, for something always is happening in this lively household.

"This is the summer shopping," said Barbara, "but I have one more day to go."

My own efforts to shop ahead for typing paper and so on really paled before this display.

"I keep one set of supplies in the kitchen," explained Barbara, "and the rest go in the cellar. I buy enough to last until Labor Day, except for meat, fresh vegetables, milk, eggs, and bread and fruit."

"But, honey, you ought to be running a grocery store!" I said, as I tried to spider myself through the wilderness of

bags. "How do you figure how much you'll need until Labor
Day?"

"I make lists," said Barbara.

As I went on down the road to have supper with my cherished Millie and Ed, I reflected that the Cape gets ready for
the summer invasion as inland we get ready for the long cold.
There must be some squirrel in all of us that suggests tucking
things away. But I could never be as efficient as Barbara, either inland or on-Cape, for I always would lose the lists, and
no matter how I plan, I end the winter at Stillmeadow with
fifteen cans of baked beans and summer on-Cape with twelve
cans of Alaskan Crab. I just do not come out even.

Ed was working in his garden as I came in and announced
happily that the peas might be in next week. This was a cold
late spring but peas are hardy. The tomato plants looked to
me a lot bigger than usual.

While we were eating one of Millie's delicious suppers, we
suddenly stopped and listened. High over the house, toward
Nauset, came the cry of the Canada geese—perhaps three
or four.

"It can't be," we all said.

But there is no sound like it.

Were they left behind or are they going to summer in
Town Cove and Duck Pond? Certainly bird habits are
changing as weather changes on this planet, but this gave us a
strange feeling of wonder. Because it was almost July!

And we just do not hear them in July. We are gentling in
to moths blundering against the picture windows, the strange
sphinx moth most spectacular, to a faintly less chorus of bird-
song beginning at five in the morning and also to less of the
closeting fogs. A heavy flooding rain this week took away
most of the pine pollen which lay in damp drifts on my road
as I went out when the storm was over. It is a mustardy-gold

color and it is too bad someone can't make beads of it for the
flower people.

On the Cape, we feel the ending of June is like listening to
a nostalgic Viennese waltz. Sentimental, it is true, but how
good to sink into sentimentality now and then! Sentiment is
honorable and rational, but sentimentality belongs to childhood emotions and pressed flowers and old love letters.

And also to me when I take the back road to Eastham to
say goodbye to the beach plums for another year and a greet-
ing to the new emerald of the salt marsh with the tidal stream
moving through it as if eternity were only a weekend.

Full summer means bumper-to-bumper crossing the bridge.
It means the beaches bearing a heavy crop of humanity. It
means campsites so full not one more car is admitted. It
means trailers and old cars made into contraptions with can-
vas tops and bunks. We have to be realistic, no matter how
we feel about the Cape, for it also means that countless people
dream of this all year, and save for it, and feel they have a
handhold on Heaven even if only for one week or two.

It means city children who learn what free running can
mean as they race up and down Skaket beach. It means parents who spread the picnic on the warm sand and feel the
tenseness of urban living drain away. It means so much to so
many that most fortunate people who never have to leave,
except for a day in Boston, feel an empathy with the invaders
in spite of the discomfort, the litter, the ghastly mess at the
dumps, the abandoned kittens and puppies and all the rest of
it.

NO VACANCY signs begin to go up early and the Information
Booth as you come into Orleans is invisible behind a wall of
cars. Summer cottages, of course, have been rented since February or since the summer before. It is no longer legal to park
by the road and sleep in the car or to simply lie down on the

beach and spend the night. Most beaches close at midnight.
The Cape economy flourishes, but the season is short and
the work hard. Most of the Cape Codders I know admit rue-
fully they would be better off financially inland, but always
add that then they would not be on the Cape. This goes along
with my feeling that Cape Cod is not a place so much as a
state of mind.

The boom in land and building began when we first came
to the Cape many years ago and provides perhaps the main
income. Eating places do well, for travelers are always hungry, but those that depend on college students for waiters
must close when colleges begin, so that is a short season, too.

It was July when we first came to the Cape and I am often
asked how it happened. All I can say is that it was fate. Fate
was my favorite cousin Rob, who persuaded us that it would
be a good idea to take some time off from work and see Cape
Cod.

Jill's children and my daughter were at camp, but somebody came in to stay with the cockers and cats at Stillmeadow. Rob and his wife, Bebe, had rented sight unseen a cottage on Champlain Road in Orleans. They drove down from
Westfield, Massachusetts, and we drove in from Southbury,
Connecticut, arriving hot and tired after six hours of driving.

One of Rob's talking points was that Jill and I had not had
any vacation in years. So we looked forward to long lazy
days on the beach and we had the back seat full of the books
we had planned to read the winter before and not had time
for.

We got to the cottage and estimated its quaint charm as we
waded through poison ivy and hay to get to the porch. What
might have been a lawn had not been mowed in years. We
learned about ticks as we went in; Jill and I had never seen a
tick. We had a good chance to observe them as we tried to

pick them off before they embedded themselves in our ankles and arms and necks.

The cottage was the typical saltbox and very old. The owner was supposed to be a direct descendant of one of the most important pirates, Pirate Tew, and I had no difficulty in believing it. The rent was astronomical for that time and charm was all the house had.

There was no electricity, just four small oil lamps with dirty chimneys and no oil. They needed new wicks. There was no plumbing and the outhouse was deep in poison ivy. There were quite a few snakes, also.

For refrigeration there was an ancient sea chest lined with tin. You bought forty pounds of ice and lugged the cake in and shut the lid down fast. A hole in the bottom of the chest let the melt go into a flat, rusty pan which always over-flowed. One skill we developed was that of perching special dishes on top of the ice cake to get really cold and not slide off into the drip.

The so-called kitchen had a two-burner oil stove, so rusty as to be doubtful as an asset. There was a lead sink with a sin-gle cold-water tap.

For furnishings, the cottage had a few wicker chairs which were not easy to sit in, and one Victorian table in the dining area. The beds had straw mattresses and flat steel springs. We found this out right away as Rob had a bad back and spent the first night wandering around muttering, "Murder! Mur-der!" He finally tried the floor and then the sofa with the broken springs. His main problem was to decide whether to try lying down at night or settle for sitting up.

The introduction to Paradise was further complicated be-cause everything was absolutely filthy. It was the first time in my life I had seen or smelled anything like it and when it be-came apparent I was rapidly getting ill, I was removed to the porch while the more stable members of the family began to scrub and scour and disinfect.

I sat and thought about our beloved Stillmeadow and would have settled for starting back that night. Why had we ever left our lovely house, box springs, refrigerator, push-button lights?

We didn't exactly rest that vacation time. Rob got a scythe and worked on the lawn. I rallied enough to wash all the odds and ends of dishes and pots and pans. Bebe and Jill rehabilitated the oil lamps and got the stove in reasonable shape. We never had time to go to the beach, we were too busy!

But by the end of the week, Rob was cooking a 7½-pound lobster over the grill we bought at Snow's. Bebe had made one of her delectable salads and we had paper plates for it. We had cool drinks with slivers of ice from that sea chest.

A cool sunset wind was rising and the smell of salt was rich in the air. The sky was that intense blue special to the Cape.

"Tomorrow I'm going up on the roof and find that leak," said Rob, twisting off a tender lobster claw.

"Tomorrow I'm going to trim back the multiflora roses," said Jill.

"Tomorrow I am going to scrub and really wax that kitchen floor," said Bebe.

"Tomorrow I am spending with the ice chest," I said. "Somehow that smell has to be stopped!"

We were not really prepared for the appearance of our landlady, who looked like something out of a Gothic tale. She was small, lean, hawk-nosed, slit-eyed. I now suspect she thought we would have complaints and believed in attack. She accused us of stealing the clothesline!

We left her to Rob, who is the mildest of men but can summon up the family temper in an emergency. I think he told her he would bill her for everything that was missing when we came, lamp shades and all.

We had a supper of leftovers that night, cold lobster, cucumber salad, warmed-up rolls, coffee. Then we rode over to Rock Harbor to watch the sunset (the car was more comfortable than the chairs anyway).

"I don't know how we could have been happier," said Jill.

"That's the way I feel," said Rob.

The next day, as I have said before, we bought a piece of land as we were leaving the Cape.

"If we come back," said Jill, "and we will come back, we are going to be in a decent house even if it is only for a weekend now and then. We pioneered when we got Stillmeadow and that was enough. We'll build a simple summer weekend cottage and this won't be any problem."

"Can we have electricity?" I asked.

"And a refrigerator," she promised.

Building a simple summer cottage is nothing to undertake lightly on Cape Cod. Perhaps in the far west prefabricated houses can go up over a weekend. It took nine months for Blue Rock to be finished. It consisted of one floor with a bedroom, a galley kitchen, a living room with fireplace, a bath with shower, no tub, a breezeway, a garage (where, of course, we never did park the car).

One of those unfolding sofa beds in the living room was my sleeping place. I loved it because the moon rose right over my head and my feet were cosied by the embers in the fireplace at night.

We did have an architect friend who could explain why adding three or four feet anywhere would double the price, and a dear builder, George Higgins, but the picture windows did not come and the fireplace flue was not finished and the pump was delayed somewhere along the line and the pine paneling was hung up off-Cape somewhere.

Finally when it was done, the *Ladies Home Journal* decorating and home staff came up to take pictures of this typical seashore cottage. We still had the aluminum trailer that Smiley Burnette had had a cowboy drive to Stillmeadow from Hollywood and we parked it in the sand. Two of the *Journal* staff slept there and I gave up the sofa bed to another. The rest stayed at a place that shall be nameless (motels had not yet blossomed every half mile) and deer mice kept them awake all night.

We picnicked and the photographer took so many color shots we lost count and we had a wonderful time! Now and then I look at those glamorous color shots and feel a full tide of nostalgia. Jill said it was all fine but then we had the problem of hauling the house trailer back to Stillmeadow, and she was right in figuring it would take about eight hours. Fortunately we had only two cockers and one Irish for that trip, because it was a rough one.

We also gave up the idea of commuting with the trailer and it never left the yard again. I used it briefly for a studio after the barn burned and now and then overflow guests slept in the twin beds. But I loved it. I always thought someday we might go adventuring and I would cook in the doll-house kitchen—

But I am not a traveling woman, probably since my whole childhood was nothing but travel. The Cape and the old farmhouse in Connecticut use up all my sense of adventure.

The typical history of Cape visitors seldom varies. First you come and spend two weeks on a vacation. Then you spend three. Then you stretch it to four. And then you begin to look for a nice inexpensive cottage or a nice inexpensive piece of land to build a little shack on.

You may buy a cottage, which naturally has no heat except some kind of kitchen stove. It may have a fireplace which does not work. The roof leaks. If there is a cellar, or half-cellar, it has been flooded.

But oh, it is yours! You have a handhold on the shining land. Your idea of dozing on the beach may never come true, but you have Gay Winds or Seaview or Land Ho. And this keeps you busy for some time.

Then comes the day you have things pretty well in shape and you sit on the terrace you have killed yourself building. Neighbors are commenting on how much you have done, and the iced drinks taste better than usual.

"Of course you could always winterize this place," says a fatal voice. "Then you could pop up for weekends in January—it never snows here . . ."

When we reached this point, we built a year-round house on the rest of the land, and this was really more practical than making Blue Rock an all-season proposition. For one thing, it is hard to dig a cellar and put a furnace in after a house is all set, especially on the Cape Cod sandy base. First you need the cellar and then the house.

The people who bought Blue Rock put in a floor furnace right in the front entry to the living room, and the first time I went over with Holly, she fell through the grating.

A typical Cape conversation goes like this: "Molly and I had this beach shack and then we felt we wanted to be able to come up whenever we felt like it—and eventually retire to the Cape. So we are getting electricity next month and insulation. But we need an extra room or so when the children come."

I have noticed in the past few years that the people who planned to spend half a year in Florida and half on the Cape tend to stay longer on the Cape and come back sooner.

House lights go on earlier in the season and yards are full of cars.

Tonight at sunset I drove over to Rock Harbor to see the fishing boats come in. The sky was a soft lemon color, for there was a cloud haze. The boats were slipping in and one already at the pier was unloading. A bronzed dark-haired fisherman was hefting a shimmering fish to an open-ended truck. I thought it was a tuna and it was at least five feet long, judging by the man's own height.

The crowd gathered to watch were quiet, even the small boys stepped softly over to look. The mystery of the sea affects man as it always has. But I also felt sad for the flashing beauty and power now ended. The bloody open gills were evidence of a last gasp for life. I told myself that fortunately I did not have to be consistent just between me and myself, for I also knew how hard the fisherman had worked for that fish and how precarious a living it now is.

So I wished the dark-haired young man well.

Rumors of Russian trawlers not far enough offshore have been persistent for some time. Occasionally one gets into trouble and we have to help out. But most of the native fishermen feel doubtful as to what kind of welcome they would have if they anchored and dragged and loaded their boats inside the twelve-mile limit off the coast of Russia.

All of us would be better off, I think, if we stayed in our own bailiwick. The United States might avoid *Pueblo* incidents (although it is a strange use of the word *incident*). The whole business of spying seems so suitable in detective fiction but there the right party always wins.

But our Anglo-Saxon temperament does not seem suited to being devious. As far back as Pearl Harbor this was obvious.

Oddly enough, along with the naïveté and simplicity our nation has, there is also a stubborn refusal to be defeated. Certainly the Revolution should never have been won by the shabby volunteer army facing the trained British troops, nor, I imagine, should the War of 1812 have ended as it did.

World War I, World War II, Vietnam—I turned and drove away from the sunset at Rock Harbor trying to start a new trend of thought. Rock Harbor Road itself comforted me, for it gives the impression of tranquillity in the garden-deep old houses and open stretch of cranberry bog and marsh in the distance. At one point you can see the marsh that lies beyond Ed Burke's house, flat as if it had been ironed and incredibly beautiful with its emerald sea-grass and little cups of pools near the tidal flow.

By the time I got across town there was just an echo of sunset on Town Cove and one ribbon of apricot over the pines beyond Mill Pond's western shore. The yard was full of quail so I waited for them. They are especially plump this year and the browns and blacks seem brighter than usual. Perhaps the amount of rain somehow has benefited them. Would more insects and seeds be easy to find?

Last week Helen Beals called me to say if I had any idea of getting the pink lilies of the valley, I better plan for it. Our friend Marian has a house in the piney woods in Eastham and a carpet of lilies of the valley too thick to find a path through. She had suggested we transplant some any time.

I found a trowel and a basket and Helen had an armful of plastic containers and a mayonnaise jar of water. It didn't look much like a professional landscaper's equipment, but we were full of enthusiasm. The back road to Eastham was quiet and sunny with the salt marshes and glimpses of the aquamarine bay beyond.

I managed to back in between Marian's pines without

Rock Harbor at sunset. (*John Schram*)

cracking a taillight. The pine needles there were three or four inches deep and walking on them is rather like jumping on a trampoline. They also are almost impossible to dig through, as we soon found out.

I had never studied pine needles before, but they seemed almost to braid themselves together and the slender tines were strong as steel. They also manage to be slippery, so both of us almost cascaded to the ground while trying to wield the trowels. It did not help that this was the first hot day we had in a long, long cold and rainy May and June.

"I wonder if July is the time to transplant these?" I asked.

"I don't have any idea," said Helen, "but I thought we had a free day."

The idea of transplanting in accord with your own schedule seemed new to me, although I am no gardener in any sense of the word. But I remember Jill arranging her whole life around when to plant what and when to fertilize and so on. She was really a slave to the gardens and trees and bushes.

This particular day it had not rained for almost a week and the ground under the pine needles was like powdered cement.

"I'm too hot," said Helen. "We better come back some other time."

"I just keep wondering if you transplant wild lilies of the valley in July," I said. "We ought to have asked that garden expert that lives near you. She knows everything."

Helen was pouring water from the mayonnaise jar onto the few raddled plants we had managed to wrest from the unyielding soil. We had four and a half after half an hour's hard work.

Then we went back to Orleans and had a cool drink and discussed John Cheever's novel, *Bullet Park*, which we both had finally read, and then I drove home with the pint plastic containers and the problem of reinterring the contents.

I had a feeling the same terrain as Marian's would be more hospitable so I found a jack pine out back that had a skirt of fallen needles. I stood on my head and dug through glacial deposit and managed to get most of the tangled roots in the same general area. It seemed to me the lilies had a tap root but the tangle of needles and other roots was not to be separated from the main plant.

The next day, fortunately, my friend David Constant turned up to try to chop back the honeysuckle from the pines it is killing. (There is nothing more feminine than this Cape wild honeysuckle. It is beautiful, it smells like the Garden of Eden, and it strangles everything within reach of the delicate tendrils.)

I showed the tiny patch of lilies of the valley to David. His narrow, sensitive face had a strange look on it. "You— planted that?" he said.

"I know it won't live," I admitted.

"It's alive today," he said firmly. "It may be hard to kill. I'll water it." He watered it heavily and has watered it three times since. So far those spear-shaped plants are well and happy.

This may prove that sometimes if you do not know anything, it works out very well anyway.

The chorus of bird song diminishes now, and Hal Borland says the bird parents are too busy to spend time singing. But my song sparrow still begins at dawn outside my bedroom window and is caroling away after sunset. And the quail keep up an endless *bobwhite* at the yard's edge.

A special sound now comes at night when the lights are on. I never draw the curtains, since the moonlight view of Mill Pond through the picture windows is like poetry remembered. A soft tapping begins first on the glass and suddenly it looks like a tapestry with the embroidery of moth-wings

pressed on the darkling panes. I stop everything to watch, for
this is a rare sight. I would not try to guess how many shapes
and sizes of moths are there from big bumbling ones to tiny
heart-shaped creatures. The prevailing color is a warm ivory,
but some are pale brown.

A problem presents itself to me. The passionate search for
the light seems to resemble the battle of the herring to get up
the herring runs to spawn. An outside lamp will, I know, be
frosted with dead bodies by daylight. Would it be better for
me to shutter the windows and quench any bit of light?
Would these fragile beings then live longer? Do the welcom-
ing lights of Still Cove lure them to death?

Or does the banging against the glass satisfy a deep urge?
Since they are night creatures, what do they do in places
where there are no lights at all? If I were not here, the only
light would be the moon and the echo of starlight over Mill
Pond. Would they fly as far as Mill Pond Road where there
is a street lamp?

If there is one firm belief I have had, it is that ascribing
human emotions to animals, birds, fish and whatever is just as
much a fallacy as saying trees writhe in agony in a storm or,
as one famous writer said recently, "the mud was evil." But I
wish I knew what the moths feel.

The rest of nature is not, fortunately, a carbon copy of
mankind. I have spent a good deal of my life trying to think
with and understand everyone from goldfish to Siamese cats,
canaries to cocker spaniels, Abyssinians to Irish setters. But I
do not expect them to give up their own identity. Instead, I
give up mine and try to think with them.

So this week I have spent most evenings trying to relate to
the moths. I do know their life-span is so brief—they are
children of summer. Some, like the gypsy moth, are deadly
enemies of man but these against my window are just a part

of hot July nights. In the morning when I go out with Amber the windowsills are dusty with them.

So, since I cannot transpose their feelings and instincts to mine, I can wonder once more about the mystery of nature. The urge to brightness is common to many species, especially man, and often man seems to feel less lost and lonely without neon lights and flashing marquees. Also on the Cape now, the beaches are jammed with people trying to incinerate themselves with sun. They yearn for it.

A good many of us, I finally decide, struggle toward some special brightness as my moths struggle toward the lamp glow and very often there is, for us, also a barrier which we may see through but cannot penetrate.

After all of my thinking, I decided to leave the lights on and the blinds up. And as the first fireflies twinkled last night at the edge of the woods, I told Amber I was not going to try to figure *them* out. I would enjoy seeing them lantern the night but I would leave it to the naturalists to interpret them!

For some reason, Amber woke me up at four-thirty the morning after I had stayed up until midnight watching the moths. I have always been fortunate with my cockers and Irish and cats; they have been willing to stay up at night and sleep half of the morning. Amber usually starts purring in my ear and poking me with her nose around ten. But this time she was dashing around and sharpening her claws on the screen and jumping around on the desk.

So I got up and double-checked the clocks to be sure it was really only four-thirty. I went to the living room and looked out of the picture windows and then I got a glass of cranberry juice and sat on the couch. The song sparrow was singing with passion. The sky over the ocean eastward was dappled with smoke-blue puffs of clouds, and behind them dawn tinted the deeps of space with a glow like the underside of a peach.

The Mill Pond was opalescent.

But what made this breathtaking was that a fine mist covered the headland and shores so except for the light from the sky the world was a dark and mysterious blur. The pines at the edge of my yard were black shadows.

It was still as only July can be. There were only two sounds, the sparrow singing and the alto note of wavelets against the shingle as the tide came in.

There was not a single moth anywhere near either big window. I almost felt I had dreamed the tapestry of wings against the glass at midnight. Two or three rabbits were thoughtfully eating the roses.

By five-thirty the shores were defining themselves and the sky toward Spain was blazing. And Amber was silhouetted against the window busily washing her paws. Her apricot fur matched the color now on Mill Pond. The triangle of her face was serene. It certainly wasn't her fault, she indicated, that I got up so early!

But she was willing to go back to bed for three more hours if I intended to!

Last evening, my friends Helen and Vicky and I drove around the back roads on the ocean side of the Cape instead of the bay side.

Down at the very end of Tonset there is a small saltbox weathered to a clove brown. Cape houses shingled with white cedar turn silvery gray, those with red cedar turn this spice-brown. The small house I asked Helen to drive by very slowly once had a sign on it and then the sign was taken down when too many visitors wanted to inspect it. This night the sign was back, no doubt owing to the historical society. The sign tells a story.

Joshua Crosby lived here and he commanded a quarter-deck gun on the frigate *Constitution* during the fight with the *Guerrière* in 1812. I assume he was not killed or there would have been an extra line on the sign. Nobody was in residence this evening so we could stop and sit and look at his house and try to visualize his farewell to his wife at the gate—was it then covered with ramblers? Were there lilacs in the door-yard?

I could see him, a small stocky man as most Cape Codders still are, with a map of wrinkles from the sea winds that almost always blow. He must have walked with the same gait the fishermen have today, slightly rolling as if to adjust to the pitch of a deck.

The light faded to a dusky lavender and the air was still and sweet with honeysuckle. And I sat wondering at the courage of these early men, fishers, carpenters, farmers, hunters, joiners (I have no idea what joiners did). They had two things in common, a passion for survival in this strange continent and a fierce determination to be free.

God bless you, Joshua Crosby. I said to myself, you did far more than fire a gun on the frigate in 1812. You left a heritage.

It is a charming small house and I hope when he got home, he raised his family in as much security as possible.

It was raining Sunday, the kind of intensely determined rain which on the Cape follows a drought. As Margaret and I drove down to Brewster, water was sliding down the steep roofs of the houses as if some aerial sluice gates had been opened. The cars were bumper to bumper, for in July on a Sunday like this, summer cottages and tents are damp and beaches are no fun.

The church where the memorial service was to be held is not the original one built on the spot, for two previous ones had burned down but it dates, I think, around 1800. It is simple, white inside and out with beautiful clear-paned windows, arched at the tops.

As we went in and sat down with Dave and Janeth Scanlon, my first feeling was that this was unreal. You may read many books about Cape Cod, the geologic history, the history of the pioneers, the wildlife, as well as countless brochures as to summer eating places, antique shops, motels, cottages, golf courses, summer theatres, drive-in movies, historic monuments.

But the Cape is not isolated from reality, for death is a part of life here as it is anywhere. Those of us gathered in the church that day were united in a single emotion which has nothing to do with time and place. We were sharing an unbearable grief at the sudden death of a twenty-one-year-old Orleans boy, just graduated from college and one whose like we were not to see again.

Now I experienced the real Cape Cod as the mourners quietly came in. I felt an identity with them all, in our sharing. There were the prosperous business leaders of the town (population: 3,000 plus, out-of-season) with well-dressed wives and children. There were schoolteachers and civic-minded people and there were summer people. There were working men wearing their best suits (wrinkled at the back where they pulled against the strong shoulders). Some relatives had driven down from Maine in the swimming highways and would be driving back the same day to spray the apple orchards if it stopped raining.

The high school friends came in small groups, only a few with their parents, most of them by themselves. They had, some of them, probably wondered whether they could be quiet and calm at this occasion. Their faces were so vulnerable as they filed in the narrow pews and bent their heads briefly. The big, sturdy boys and slim girls with mists of fall-

ing golden hair were not intimate with death as the parents
and older people were. The overall weight of grief in our
world had had no power yet over their particular dreams.

For a good many, this was an introduction to disaster and
they came to face it together, gathering some comfort from
being close to one another. It was my first sight of the Orleans nineteen- and twenty-year-olds and I, too, found comfort in it.

I would have liked a photograph of them as an antidote to
the magazine color shots of teenage LSD victims and screaming student rioters smashing files in a dean's office.

Very little has been done for the young in Orleans, and
there was then no youth center which they could manage
themselves, with a place to drink soft drinks, play guitars,
sing and dance. During the time Richard was here, his family
kept open house, but few houses are big enough to be a permanent clubhouse. Now the youngsters were silent.

The sound of the insistent rain made a blurred background
for the organ music. Otherwise it was still. There was no
coughing or shifting about, just silence like the bottom of a
well.

When the service was over, the mourners filed quietly out
into the downpour and faced the prospect of the traffic as the
vacationers drove bumper to bumper trying to find something to do, since the beaches were impossible. Cars full of
children and dogs, and cars dragging boats and trailer campers with small faces pasted against every window—they all
went by and then the policemen stopped traffic to let the cars
from the church get on the road.

For all life is a merging.

When I got home, I sat down to look out at Mill Pond
with Amber in my arms. Her small heart beat steadily against
my hand and she put her velvet-soft arms around my wrist

and polished me with her sandpaper tongue, purring all the while. We sat for a long time while I tried to re-establish some sort of meaning in the universe.

We are intimate with death in this period as we have not been since World War II. Our rendezvous with history has been a grievous one. Last week the total Vietnam casualties were way over 42,000 and by now, the end of July, will be more. These are the young with lifetimes ahead, barring becoming statistics. When the newsmen announce very light casualties, only 100 or so, I am thinking that even one death is too much.

Richard was not yet in service, having just graduated from college at twenty-one. His older brother, Peter, had been two years in the navy, stationed in the Vietnam area, and was flown back for the funeral. Richard himself was the innocent victim of an instantaneous automobile accident.

This brings up the eternal why, and acceptance is the basic problem of humanity. The only answer for most of us is a faith in an everlasting power which many of us call God. Our very need, I think, implies there is an answer to it. I used to visualize God as looking like my grandfather, with curly white hair, a white rich beard and sea-blue eyes. My grandfather was, indeed, a deity to his family and I was quite grown-up before I decided God was not a copy of Grandpa.

Now there is the problem of space being conquered so we cannot think of a neat Heaven beyond the moon with God walking amid immortal flowers. But I personally reach out to a bigger concept which I cannot define. I feel when I pray that my prayers do not vaporize in air. I feel a strengthening of my spirit.

Twilight diminished the rain this Sunday and the drought-sered grass was already greening. Mill Pond was pewter and one pale candle of light shone in the sky. And all at once I felt a presence, an everlasting support overpowering death as I prayed.

The worst heat wave usually comes toward the end of July. When it hits the Cape, nobody can believe it. In the middle west, where I grew up, this was expected. It belonged to corn-growing weather. When I visited Jill, my college roommate and lifelong friend, in Freeport, Illinois, I went in July. We used to spread sheets on the parlor floor at night and try to sleep on them. If it got down to 90°, that was better. In my home in Appleton, Wisconsin, a breeze from the river below our house sometimes came up late at night.

But Cape Cod is not supposed to *ever*, ever get really hot. Surrounded by water, it stays warmer in winter and cooler in summer. It is ideal. However, there is one heat wave that always manages to come across the bridge.

It is a personal insult to every true Cape Codder and to those of us who spend more than a quick vacation here.

I am particularly vulnerable since I have a number of windows which cannot be opened and several have the storm glass on all year. Today when it was over ninety, I got out the electric fan and plugged it in, in the living room. Then I went into the wing and started to type. A sudden noise made me think guests were dropping in and I went back to the front of the house. The whole living room smelled of burned rubber, hot oil and disaster. Fortunately, the fuses had not burned out. But the fan was ready for the dump.

It is invariably true that any appliance I have always gives up dramatically at the worst possible moment. The furnace inland goes off when it is thirty below zero, never during the January thaw. The electric range went off last Christmas as dinner was cooking for the family. The vacuum cleaner collapsed after a party when the floors were deep with crumbs.

So naturally the fan gave out on the hottest day of summer.

At the same time the radio reported that all of the east coast was faced with a power shortage and everyone must turn off air-conditioners and all electric appliances possible or there would be no electricity at all. I think it was 1966 when this last happened and we all felt that the shortage would be taken care of in a couple of years!

Refrigerators do not stay cold too long and freezers start defrosting, and restaurants and ice cream stands suffer greatly. Our whole lives, actually, are based on electric current. Orleans has town water now, but I have my sweet-water crystalline well and that, of course, implies the pump going to pump it up.

So I drew a few pans and pitchers of water, just in case, filled the ice bucket and planned to eat out of cans if the electricity went off rather than venture to open the refrigerator door. The refrigerator was jammed with crabmeat, chicken, flounder fillets. The freezer section had spinach soufflé, crab Newburg, creamed chipped beef, cheese soufflé.

Of course the week before I had been clearing everything out and there had been only eggs, butter, milk and a few vegetables in it. But now I was all stocked up.

I washed the dishes in the sink, decided against starting the dishwasher in case the current went off in mid-cycle. Then I sat down and read *The Andromeda Strain* while reflecting that civilization is not always a complete blessing!

In the early days on Cape Cod, rain water was collected in barrels and carried to the house in buckets as needed. It couldn't have been too sanitary but, as someone pointed out, people lived to be ninety in that period. Cooking was done on cast-iron stoves, and in winter the parlor stove was set up and fed with chunks of wood. In summer, the parlor stoves were taken out and the tinsmith repaired them. Oil lamps

gave a mellow light and handmade bayberry candles a sweet
spicy scent as they burned.

It was a hard life, for even very young children had to help
the family, but families were united in the business of living
and there are times when I do not think we should feel so su-
perior with all of our technology.

The Cape sky is still clear except when the dump burns,
and the water is as yet unpolluted except in certain areas
where sewage seeps in. It is something of a miracle, since Boston is less than two hours' driving time away, Providence is
not much farther and even New York City is less than a
day's trip. We know now how precious clean air is—
having taken it for granted most of our lives as well as water
safe to swim in and to drink.

Every season the past few years, however, I see men on
Mill Pond beach taking samples to be sure this quiet stretch
of water has not been contaminated. They take shellfish too
for examination.

Wildlife is less abundant than when I first came, but two
young deer played in my yard summer before last and pheasant and quail are everywhere.

Every day there is some change as July ebbs. This afternoon Amber and I went out for a walk and I noticed for the
first time that the Scotch broom has gone to seed, the fountain of lemon-colored blooms gone. But in their place the
seedpods hung from the slender spires and they were pale
lavender, like twilight. They are slender and pointed at the
tips, and they mark the change of season with a different kind
of beauty.

Amber was too busy nibbling special grass tips to bother
with them. Her world is on a different level from mine, for

she is small and finds even short grass is like a jungle. She tip-toes as we go along but keeps her nose busy, for she uses her sense of smell like a hunting dog and every tiny buttercup gets a thorough going over. Where there is a late rose, she stands as tall as she can and sniffs with delight, petal after petal.

She also tracks. I can tell exactly where a neighboring dog has moved across the lawn or a rabbit hopped on his way to eat the last of my annuals.

The yellow snapdragon, which we used to call butter-and-eggs, has begun to bloom and Amber had to sniff every upturned cup. Something new, she said, switching her tail! Next to it is an unnamed feathery green bush which she likes to nibble, and I explain we do not eat things just because they are there. A good many ordinary plants are poison to cats and some also to children; the Boston radio this summer has a list of dangerous plants, most of them ordinary.

The Full Buck Moon of July swings over Mill Pond and cool air comes through the open windows, smelling of salt and seaweed. There is a soft lapping of the tide like an obbli-gato to the music of the night. The moon track on the dark water is definite enough to make me want to walk on it, dip-ping my feet in pure gold.

Perhaps the greatest gift of the Cape is the intimacy we have with sky and sea and shining sands, and as we enter the space age we shall be more grateful than ever for this narrow land where the tides are not regulated by computer and the skyway travelers are the wild geese going over and the red-wings announcing spring and the seagulls swooping against the fire of sunset.

Queen Anne's lace and day-lilies take over as the roses go. Wild blackberries ripen. Daisies bloom and petunias spread

color in every dooryard. Hydrangeas love the salt air and
sandy soil and the bushes bend with the weight of rich blue-
purple blossoms. All they need, says Ed Connors, is water
and water and water.

My two small ones lie flat if the water is not there regularly. Then with a good soaking, they spring up in phoenix
fashion. Most of the time, people with gardens pray for rain
in July and the vacationers pray for beach weather.

The only time Cape Codders feel there is enough rain, I
notice, is when the cellars are flooded and sump pumps are
going full tilt. Otherwise they say it is raining too hard and it
will all run off, or it isn't raining hard enough and the water
will not penetrate more than a quarter of an inch.

I always say that any rain at least washes off the leaves.

This particular July will go down in history as the time
that man landed on the moon. Perhaps this offsets the fact
that twenty-four years ago the first A-bomb was exploded in
the desert in New Mexico!

In July the two most noticeable signs on the Cape are for
lobster pools and chowder houses. Many fish markets sell
chowder base, and chowder is on every menu, for it is not a
winter soup here. It is basic.

I notice at the Lobster Claw on the hottest summer day,
most visitors order clam chowder! Actually it is quahog
chowder, and summer residents usually dig their own for it,
which is called scratching.

The early settlers who invented clam chowder out of what
they had on hand did a better job than many gourmet cooks
of today! Quahogs were only a shell-toss away, salt pork
was always on hand, potatoes for the digging, and milk. Pepper, of course, was scarce, since it came in by sailing ship, but
they were not used to having it on the table daily.

Summer's lease is all too short and in four more weeks the trip back across the bridge will begin for so many. Already the clearance sales begin all over the narrow land and early fall clothes are coming into the shops. But we are an impatient people and of late years start putting up Christmas decorations in November! We tend, I think, to live ahead too much.

I prefer to live each day as fully as possible, but I find myself swept along with the *Cape Codder* advertising from the gift shops that suggest this is a fine time to buy your Christmas presents and order the Christmas cards.

The landscape man, who comes when it suits, has spent much time chopping out poison ivy and clearing the weeds from the steps to the beach before the grandchildren arrive in August and is already planning that in late fall he will cut more brush and take out two cedars that are choking each other (just half-trees, he says, I better take them out). He will then put in more bulbs, everything except the tulips which the rabbits devour like invading hordes.

So he, too, is living ahead.

This July ends with five days of cloudy, cold, nonbeach weather and I hear a good many campers in Nickerson Park have given up and started home. The rain falls intermittently in a lacy pattern against my windows. And yesterday Bob Snow called up to say the man would be around shortly to clean the furnace. When he left, he had turned the furnace on and the warm glow of heat was pleasant so I left it on for an hour or so and Amber was delighted to stretch full-length by the baseboard grid and spread her toes in and out and purr.

But fresh corn is being brought across the bridge daily and ripe tomatoes are $1.69 cents for two pounds, and very soon Ed Connors will have his garden full of them. So it is still midsummer!

For eighty-seven years, more or less, Snow's has been a focal point in Orleans. It is an ancient irregular building with worn white clapboards and was shaded by the elegance of elms until last summer when the elms were cut down. The trunks were thick enough to build a cottage in.

Snow's is called a hardware store simply because it is indescribable. In the cool shadowy basement you trip over stacked cartons as you hunt for household supplies, china, glass, pots and pans, bathmats, curtain rods, lamps and lampshades. Upstairs there is a paint section, a side with tools, dog collars and wild bird seed, as well as fertilizer and beach umbrellas and NO TRESPASS signs.

The west end houses toys and toys and toys, stereo records, stationery and the confusion of gifts summer people buy to take back across the bridge. There is also room, somehow, for a washing machine, electric range, dryer, toasters and percolators.

There are no groceries, shoes or clothing, but the stock answer to any visitor who asks where to get anything else is, "Have you tried Snow's?"

The men and women who work there seem to care greatly whether you get the right pencils or the shade of paint you need. It is pleasant to visit with them the way people visit in a social club.

This week the *Cape Codder* ran a drawing of the way Snow's will look after it is remodeled. The town was in a state of complete shock. The long efficient modern building, said the newspaper, would be built behind the present edifice. It looked much like a modern factory. The present store would be torn down and replaced by an ample parking lot (as if any parking lot could ever be ample enough!).

The Snow brothers explained that they must expand, much as they deplored the necessity. Well, it is true the windows are so jammed with merchandise that they look as if a tornado had just been by. And it is difficult to get from one spot to another inside, steering a dubious course around everything.

It is also true, as most of us admit, that nothing can be done to prevent the change from a peaceful Cape village to a bustling town, eventually city. I don't doubt when the land is all filled, piers will stretch out into the impassive ocean and more buildings will go up.

But those of us who love Orleans do not have to be happy about this. We would be perfectly happy digging around in Snow's forever, just to have it the same as it has been down the long years.

The idea of keeping the personality of a town is new, just as the idea of conserving our natural resources is new. We erase the vestiges of the past without a backward look, seeking more efficiency, more money. Historic houses are bulldozed down for new throughways. It costs too much to move them, say the experts, while pouring millions into roads to move traffic faster and faster.

Snow's cannot help moving, it is the way of the times. But how sad it is! And sadder that the 30,000 summer people who seek the release from cities bring the seeds of change with them, as the Pilgrims brought England's seeds, including weeds, in the *Mayflower*.

I was reviewing all this as I took my list to Snow's last Wednesday. Wednesday is the day it is closed, and invariably I need to get something there on a Wednesday. The old-fashioned window shades are pulled down, the ancient door padlocked. Snow's has been closed on Wednesdays ever since I can remember, but every week I start out to get something there on Wednesday.

I somehow hope that in the elegant new building, Snow's will still be closed on Wednesdays, so one thing at least will be the same. And I hope the electric-yellow oil trucks will still roll out as reliably as always.

Listening to Cape conversation, I think there is a cross-section of every variety of accent in this country. Cape Cod has drawn people from everywhere, who have felt the lure of this narrow land and eventually managed to move here. In time, what the real Cape Codders call foreign accents smooth over but nobody can copy or approximate the true Cape speech. About the only thing you can say is that there is no *R* in this alphabet, and since the sound of *R* is homely at best, the deletion is an advantage. Cape Codders speak in quiet voices mostly and the sentence rhythm is gentle.

A talk with a real Cape Codder rests the spirit.

When a small group gathers before a driftwood fire, it is more stimulating than a top theatre production. The assertive, quick, city speech melded with the soft, flat Cape voices makes a tapestried effect which is delightful.

At such times art and music and world affairs and the problems of education in this country remind me of a postgraduate seminar. The amount of reading done in this narrow land is staggering.

When I try to analyze all types of talk on the Cape, I think I come up with the answer. One answer is, of course, that one can go into the deep south, as I have, or the great middle west or the eastern cities, it is not difficult to capture the essence of the place in the talk and simply copy it down. But the Cape is different. I believe, after much thought, that the superficial party talk one often does hear has deep roots in the tragic happenings in this world. Women gathered for a coffee hour or men having cocktails want to have an interval of plain ordinary peace. Weather and birds, or where the fish are biting (for the men), bring a temporary release and an illusion that the world is rocking along as usual. Without illusion, we are lost.

On the other hand, the gatherings for serious thinking provide a sharing of anxiety which we hunger for. And perhaps one reason I love Cape Cod so deeply is that communication with my fellow men provides both kinds of sustenance.

The caste system on the Cape is simple. If your ancestors were here, you belong to the elite. Some people who have lived here all their lives and raised their children here may be an integral part of Cape society, but someone eventually says they come from Boston or Springfield. They are from across the bridge. A third category consists of people who spend much of the year here but go south with the birds to escape the harsh winter. Then there are the summer people.

The summer people pour in and lift the economy of the Cape but jam the roads and change the natural pace of living.

And I admit one of the best moments of my life was when a true Cape Codder said, "I'm glad you could get heah befoah the summer people come. Nice and quiet now."

When I go over my statements about the Cape, I realize they cannot be adequate, for the Cape is too complex to index in any way. Actually the *only* thing one can be positive about is that the Cape Cod accent is unlike any other.

Nevertheless I keep on trying to share what I feel about the Cape. For the sense of being indigenous to it must somehow be shared. So many people feel it.

"The first time we crossed the bridge, I suddenly felt I was coming home," said a friend of mine. "It was the strangest feeling—we just came for a week just because we had never seen it. And we've been here eleven years now."

"We always planned to live in California," said another, "but we drove up from New York on a holiday weekend. Here we are."

"Of course Ralph had to take a steep cut in pay," said a third. "Cape doesn't pay too much. But we talked it over and began to pack up."

This cannot be due to the beauty of the sea, for our country has seashores in many places. It is not the pine-deep woods or shining beaches or even the sense of history which clings to every town. It is, I think, a quality in the people, in the way life is lived. Perhaps Cape Cod is not a place, but a state of mind, as I have often said.

Here, as everywhere, there are mean and small-minded folk. There is plenty of intolerance and bias but there is also a community sense. When trouble strikes, the response is universal.

When the father of nine children was crushed to death by a falling beam, those who scarcely knew him began to work for the fund for the children. When an elderly woman fell ill, her house was invaded by people with casseroles and custards. And when the beloved twenty-one-year-old boy was killed, everyone in town accepted it as a personal grief. I noted voices were lowered and people moved slowly along the street for some days.

And when the herb lady was taken to the hospital by ambulance for her final ride, one of the grocery girls came out to my car as I parked it.

"I thought I would tell you," said Marge, "so you could send a card."

Another unusual quality I have found on the Cape is a lack of discrimination against the aged. People do seem to live longer, perhaps because of the lack of nervous tension and maybe a little less preoccupation with financial success. But when someone is "carried off" at ninety, few remark that it was time she went. They still think it was too bad life ended. Older people are regarded as people here and not a nuisance to be discarded as rapidly as possible.

Possibly this attitude helps keep the aging a part of society. It is good not to be ashamed of being eighty-five. The cult of the young has not yet overflowed this area. It may be the bomb-throwing militant youngsters may change this, but so far they have not done so.

When I heard a Panther on television the other night predict that everything was going to be blown up, there wouldn't be any work or any money, just places full of LSD, I felt sure he had never been to Cape Cod. Instead of being on national television and on magazine covers, I reflected, he would have been better off working at a nonincendiary job and taking the weekend for fishing or water-skiing or just walking the dunes and sensing the immensity of the ocean.

When I called the plumber one morning last March to report a strange noise from the pump, I had a pleasant visit with his wife. He couldn't come for a week because everyone wanted their water turned on now. The season was beginning earlier every year.

"Used to be May first," she said. "Now it's March and they're coming."

I thought of the cottages that had been closed and silent all winter, tucked away in the dunes, hidden down winding pine-dark roads, stark against the pale winter sky on lonely glacial ridges. Houses are, after all, extensions of the families that inhabit them, and a closed house makes the heart sad. I was happy to think of the water turned on, the electricity operating and open doors letting out the damp must of winter. My own pump still labored away and after all had me as a companion, so it didn't really matter how soon Larry came.

My own house is never shut up for winter. It gives me the feeling that it isn't so lonesome. My dear neighbors Millie and Ed come over to check. The refrigerator purrs along, the furnace grumbles as usual, and hot water runs from the faucets.

When I leave Stillmeadow, at the other end, the children move in and the house is full of everything from rabbits to archeologists. So the old farmhouse is happy. In the language of today, it swings!

There are two opposing opinions both on the Cape and inland as to the benefit of closing a house. Most of us (meaning those who agree with me) feel that things rust and mildew and chair-rungs come unglued when a house is closed. Mice get in, occasionally a raccoon will gnaw up the kitchen table or squirrels eat the mattresses. Somehow if a house is not closed tight and someone comes in and out, less dire things occur.

The opposing camp believes it is too expensive to keep a furnace going and it wears out the refrigerator and so on, not to mention that there is danger of fire.

To each his own.

Autumn

I SHALL REMEMBER

I met two girls that silvery rainy night
They wore the raindrops as they welcomed me.
September grass grew delicate and light
Near the pale roses leaning toward the sea.
Scattering quail fled soft as falling leaves,
For Autumn lay across the narrow land.
And hearts accept—they must—but summer grieves
Abandoning again the blessed strand.

The house gave steady open testament
That much endures as seasons ebb away,
Wide-open doors, warm lights shone eloquent
Welcome for those who stopped—so brief a stay.

Summer is over, but tonight I shall remember
Two girls, the rain, and roses in September.

Summer slides so gently into autumn on Cape Cod that it is easy to believe there will be no end. Day dreams toward twilight, skies are sapphire, the tide ebbs quietly. I begin to think time itself is arrested and the green leaves will stay forever on the trees. Gardens glow with color, with late roses and with carpets of zinnias and asters.

After Labor Day, the procession of summer people moves toward the bridge. Some of them stay on into October, but those with children in school or college must pack up and go, and then begin counting the months until they can come back. Orleans itself settles into her own routine. Parking space opens up on Main Street, cars no longer wait in line at the gas stations, and the laundry window no longer says fiercely, "No more drys—and this does mean you!"

Sandwich and ice cream stands are boarded up before long and alas, Philbrick's shack on Nauset beach closes the wooden shutters. Those who stay on in Orleans rush to Nauset for a few last rounds of fried clams, fried shrimp, and French-fried onions as only Philbrick does them. You order your lunch or supper and carry it back to the car in convenient containers. Most people can eat a pint of the fried onions, all the time discussing how they are done—so crisp, nongreasy, sweet. Even nononion eaters munch them happily. The general opinion is that the onions are perfect in the first place and deep fried in pure freshly heated fat which is never, never reused. They have an almost lacy texture, translucent when you pick up a savory circle.

The Lobster Claw and Lobster House are still crowded while everyone tries to visit them before they also close. We always hope they will stay open until the first of November, and it is a melancholy day when the signs go up—CLOSED.

The Inn stays open all winter, which is a great relief. This is a rambling shapeless building at the edge of the Town Cove. I think it has been added to for many years. Now the most notable feature is a purple turret poking up from the roof. The pleasant dining rooms hang right over the water and at sunset one can "sip one's favorite cocktail," as they always say, while watching the cove waters turn apricot. I have a special feeling for the Inn, since it was the first place Jill and I went to for dinner when we decided to buy the land.

The girls who wait on table, Jeannine and Bernice, are special friends and Mr. Martin, the current owner, comes in to visit while the roast is served. Alice and Anne, my granddaughters, love to go there because they can run downstairs and be right on the shore and still get back in time for their chocolate parfaits.

The Lobster Claw is a favorite meeting place for lunch, and Eileen DeLory and I meet there often. If we are lucky, Jimmy slips in on his noon hour. A lovely waitress, oddly also called Jimmy, is always on hand looking daisy-fresh and pretty no matter how jammed the place is.

The Lobster House is run by Lois and Webb Eldredge, and they specialize in gourmet dining. Nothing will cure a depression faster than Webb's baked stuffed crab legs or beef tenderloin en brochette with pilaf. I finally learned this season how he serves celery sticks so crisp they crunch. He soaks them in ice water overnight.

Surf casting for stripers, Nauset Beach. (*John Schram*)

There is a story about the third dining house. It is on the bay side of Orleans, near Skaket, and was once a magnificent mansion, rather like something in a southern romance, with pillars, a garden with a pool and fountain, wisteria in clouds of purple at the entrance. I was in it once before it was changed into the Captain's Club, and longed to write a book about those who had moved up and down the stately stairs and sat in the walled gardens. I still think of them as I eat the famous lobster bisque which the club features.

Several smaller eating places, such as Helen's Kitchen, stay open, but Mayo's outdoor barbecue stand closes when Mayo's main emporium ends the season. I cannot call Mayo's anything but *emporium*, for it is stocked with baked goods of all sorts, frozen casseroles, barbecued duckling (now weekends on order only), sandwiches, lobster rolls, chocolate and plain milk. When a harried housewife finds out seven relatives are dropping in for supper, the equally harried husband is dispatched to Mayo's on the double.

"Just get everything for supper—be sure enough for nine."

He may come home with clam pie, or chicken pie, or beef stroganoff and probably on his own, potato salad and cole slaw! Plus the famous squash rolls.

Of course the Cape is full of delightful eating places in season, from Hyannis to Provincetown, but one thing I never would attempt is to write a guide to good eating, having had one dire experience recommending the best places in Connecticut some years ago for a booklet put out by a foundation. Unfortunately it took some time for it to be printed and by the time it came out EVERY single one of the places I had praised had changed hands and was not fit to mention. I had a lot of very critical mail that season.

Now I suggest people try for themselves and make their own list.

Wherever you go, from the cranberry houses to the out-door grill stands, you may always quaff a glass of the state's official drink (as of last April), which is cranberry juice. Some people like the idea of thinking that the Indians, three hundred and fifty years ago, used cranberries to make their pemmican, a staple of their diet. Some health-minded folk love the idea of all that Vitamin C which is not in pill form. But most visitors enjoy the refreshing tang and glowing color, and most year-rounders keep a quart or so always in the refrigerator. It is one of the nicest gifts Cape Cod has given, and the 757,000 barrels of cranberries produced last year came to a happy use.

One of the busiest places in town now is Nickerson's Lumber Company. Everyone who is building wants to get "roofed in" before bad weather sets in. The big trucks travel every road loaded with sweet-smelling lumber, rolls of insulating material, thermopane window glass and tons and tons of nails. And kitchen units. I have a feeling of being related to Nickerson's in some way since my dear friend Ed Connors works there. If I ever get in serious trouble, I can always call Nickerson's and leave a message for Ed.

Nickerson's Lumber Company is on Main Street in Orleans, although it has additional centers in Chatham, Wellfleet, West Dennis, Hyannis and Pocasset. Nickerson's is seventy-five years old and is currently administered by Joshua Nickerson, Jr., of the third generation.

The founder, Oscar C. Nickerson, went to sea when he was fourteen, as was quite proper, and was a captain at twenty-one. He was one of eleven children and had his own way to make. When he was about twenty-eight, he scraped together and borrowed enough money to purchase a failing lumber business in Chatham. The price was $4,250.

Last year, I am informed, the gross was seven and three-quarter million dollars. This success story began with faith and hard work and a vision of the future. Captain Nickerson evidently learned about lumber as his ship carried cargoes of it. Transporting lumber was economical and the market grew as the Cape developed. The railroad came in 1887 and made a stop in West Chatham. Summer visitors went by horse and buggy from the station to their summer residences, or to hotels, where ladies could sit in wicker rocking chairs on shady verandas or, if they were daring, play croquet on the croquet green.

By the time the railroad failed, the Cape was booming and building required lumber. Soon the one-room schoolhouse such as Joshua Nickerson attended was abandoned. Along with it went houses heated by wood stoves and outdoor privies and the tin tub for the Saturday-night bath. The iceman hauling cakes of ice in his wagon was superseded by electric refrigeration. Drugstores took over for the Larkin wagon filled with patent medicines that would cure anything. More churches were needed.

It all took lumber and building supplies. Today Nickerson's windows have a dazzling display of everything from aluminum sash to furniture and carpeting, and Nickerson trucks roll daily as do the white automobiles with *Nickerson* signed in blue on their sides. The model house named Abel W. Parker is the only reminder of the beginning of this empire, since the first ship Oscar Nickerson sailed was the Abel W. Parker.

Smith's hardware and Bessom's country store have a long heritage also, and it is heartening to think of our country as built on individual enterprise instead of the rigid structures of a communist regime!

Across the road and to the right of Snow's stand the three Nickerson prebuilt Cape Cod houses which attract a steady stream of visitors all summer. Naturally they are named Cap-

tain Eldredge, Abel W. Parker, Cape Codder. The inside
plan may be adjusted to meet the needs of the purchaser, and
you might even put two houses together for a bigger residence. As we drive along the gentle country roads, I like to
identify the Nickerson homes and see how they look with
gardens and lawns and clotheslines in back yards and lamps in
front windows.

Which reminds me that it is the custom here to have lamps
in the front windows. My reason tells me this cannot be a
heritage from the early days when lanterns were lit to guide
fishermen home, and candles burned through cold foggy
nights, but I like to think it is anyway. In any case, it is a
heartwarming sight to see the windows glowing with the
golden light of lamps. Any homecoming mariner from the
daily battle with life has a welcome waiting.

The few houses, and there are some, which draw down the
blinds or draw the curtains as dark falls, always bring a comment from someone.

"Wonder what's wrong with Mrs. S? Scared somebody'll
know she's at home?"

"You know there's something queer about the B's. Only
light you can see in that house at night is through a crack in
the front door."

"No, I don't know the new family up the hill. Can't be
very friendly, never a peep of light out of that house."

We all know change is the way of life, but on Cape Cod
there is always the underlying fear that the Cape *might* just
get to be like any other place. Change comes in many ways,
some of them small. For instance, up to a few years ago almost nobody ever felt it necessary to lock up the house if the
family went on a picnic. When we called for a service man,
we said, "Tell him to walk right in. I won't be home but he
knows where the TV set is."

Then I noticed a good many people graduated to, "I leave the key under the loose shingle by the back door. Tell him to put it back after he fixes the refrigerator."

My friends Helen and Vicky are used to urban living in New Jersey, and when they came summers to the Cape made a great thing of locking the cottage every time they went swimming. Since they invariably locked themselves out, it was a good thing I had a spare key and, of course, my own house was never locked, so they could come right in and retrieve their own key.

Most of us still, however, leave the house open so the milkman can come in and put the milk in the refrigerator and the groceryman can tuck the frozen items in the freezing compartment.

Locking the car is another miserable sign of the times. The first time I was induced to lock mine was when Ruth Walker and Charlotte Webber advised it for a sound reason. Holly was inside and they felt some stranger might covet her. I managed to get it locked and we went to the Ranch House for an elegant dinner, during which a terrible rainstorm came up—and they come faster on the Cape than anywhere I have ever lived. We came out and sloshed to the car in our light summer frocks. Holly jumped up and down with joy. And then, of course, I could not get a single door open! There was evidently sand in the locks. I have seldom felt more miserable as the torrents came down and Holly pressed her nose to the glass of each door and I battled it. In the end, one door gave in.

I solved this problem once and for all. I never locked the car doors again. I do take the ignition keys out and drop them in my shopping basket. This means that I must empty the basket to find them, for keys have a way of hiding. If I make any expensive purchases, I make them just before I go home so they are not left in the car when it is parked on

Main Street. It's all a question of management, as my dear veterinarian always says about Amber and her various food phobias.

I think the dependence on locks arose when a few of the most verbal hippies and other young folk began to say on TV that everything belongs to everybody and you should take anything you want. It is not stealing, said one handsome twenty-year-old, because everything is in common.

In any case, I notice some residents now take their best lawn chairs in the house if they are going away for a weekend. And nobody leaves the oars in a rowboat nowadays. Sunfish sails are lugged home from Mill Pond and small boat motors heaved up the banks to the cars at the top.

On the big beaches people keep a wary eye on the umbrellas, and in the supermarkets someone guards the bulging baskets of food.

Along with this goes a need for identification if you go to a bank to cash a check. A few years ago some men came over the bridge from Boston and did a big business cashing forged checks at most of the banks. Now the banks want to be sure, and one sometimes feels the tellers must have known your grandparents before you in order to honor a twenty-five-dollar check. I admit this does give one a kind of glow when a check is cashed without any question! It's like belonging to the Ivy League.

The landscape is changing so rapidly that a new road may appear between one day and the next. Whole stretches of woodlands are leveled as developments go up. But there is yet enough of the old Cape to be the heart's home for many of us.

As yet we have no house numbers, although the rumor is that this change may come. In Orleans, on Cape Cod, we are tired of figures and numbers. Beginning with social security, we have account numbers, all sorts of serial numbers, charge-card numbers, bank safety-deposit numbers. There is a strong sense of identity on the Cape. People want to belong to names not digits.

I definitely resist the idea of my house being number three on Blue Rock Road. I want it to be called the last house before the road runs into the woods. I want it known as Still Cove.

It is fashionable to put quarterboards on houses with a name on them. My neighbor's house is Tick Tock Hill and not yet number two. Tick Tock Hill establishes the house as a personality, and since the owner collects antique clocks, it is most suitable. The quarterboard on Morrison's defines the home as Braemar—Bill is Scotch.

When we came to the Cape, some people were fortunate enough to have authentic old quarterboards from honest ships, and they are almost priceless now. A house we stayed in earlier had a lovely one, all carved and gilded, and it was QUEEN OF NAUSET. I have seldom coveted anything as much as I did that venerable quarterboard.

Now there are men who make fake quarterboards which say everything from Sunset View to Gay Winds. They do very well. My favorite place name is Sea Call Farm, which belongs to the flower lady on Tonset. Then there is Quail Hollow—but obviously no fishing boat was ever named Quail Hollow—or Lilac Farm, for that matter!

I like to drive around Orleans just looking at the house names and thinking about the folk who live there. And all the time I wish I had Queen of Nauset on my own house! But oddly enough I do not want a copy, I want the original.

Still Cove was named because Mill Pond is like a cove really, and although she can be wild as El Greco's "View of Toledo" at times, she is often still and full of serenity. Then, too, there is a link with the inland farm, Stillmeadow.

Some summer cottages, alas, have names like Dunrovin or Cumin. This can't be helped. However, I can see why my own cousin Rob considers their place should be named Bagg's Folly, for they have had a series of disasters in the restoration of the charming old house. They may settle for the more customary Bayberry Knoll or Blueberry Hill or some version of the ever present cranberry.

In May I drive past one house that should be called Shadblow, for the drifts of snowy blossoming shadblow frame it with delicate beauty.

I must mention a second Cape custom with regard to homes. Gilded wooden eagles glare over garage doors, front entry ways, or just under the curve of the roof line. With spread wings and predatory beaks, they add a special Cape signature. A few of these, too, are antiques, most are accurate copies.

Road names on the Cape are delightful. Many of them are Indian and many echo the past, like Barley Neck Road, Pochet, Twiss Road, Defiance Lane, Rock Harbor Road. My part of town is Tonset, and I hope the long-gone Tonset Indian chief knows his name is remembered.

There is one whole town called Mashpee, and it is the home of the descendants of the original Mashpee Indians, who are still an independent citizenry. I have been told this is the only entirely Indian community outside of reservations. They have an annual Indian festival which attracts many visitors but most of the time they go about the business of living. It is sad to think that the land has only one surviving Indian community when it once belonged entirely to the friendly tribes without whose help the Pilgrims would have perished.

Sometimes I speculate as to the course of history. Suppose the Pilgrims had not survived the starvation winters? Suppose the three small ships had never even reached this alien shore?

And suppose there had never been the Revolution? Even the most astute historian cannot answer these questions!

The Full Harvest Moon of September shines so brightly I have the illusion I could read by it. If the house lights inside are turned off, the moonlight casts shadows of the window bars against the opposite walls and the carved whales over the fireplace seem to float on their own shadows. Mill Pond gives off light.

Hal Borland tells me at one time farmers went back to the fields after supper and worked by moonlight, and I remember during my young schooldays in Wisconsin that my father was always restless on bright September nights and charged around in the yard like a misdirected rocket. Mamma and I would be washing the supper dishes and hear him crashing around.

"Goodness knows what he's doing this time," Mamma would say. "I hope he doesn't upset the neighbors!"

No doubt Father was echoing his own childhood. He was one of eight children, four boys and four girls, and Grandpa owned an enormous farm along the river in West Springfield, Massachusetts. I am sure no Bagg ever sat down in those days except to eat a light meal of roast beef, baked potatoes, gravy, fresh vegetables, apple pie and ice cream. Breakfast was country sausage or home-cured bacon and eggs or sugary basted ham, fried potatoes and apple pie, aided by fresh hot buttery rolls. This kept one's strength up.

Times have changed but the Harvest Moon exerts the same magic. I have no outside work to do on the Cape by moonlight but I feel restless, not ready to give day up and finish indoor tasks. Many a September night my Irish and I have driven to Nauset to see the shining spindrift and then to Rock Harbor on the bayside to see the old lightship against the luminous sky. The fishing boats that are at anchor in the

Fireplace at Still Cove. (*John Schram*)

channel nudge the piling softly, perhaps dreaming of tomorrow.

People with small vegetable gardens are busy bringing in the crops just in case there is an early frost, although frost is usually late on the Cape. How good the last glowing tomatoes are! And there is so much squash! The last loads of fruit and vegetables are trucked in across the bridge for the roadside stands, and the smell of sweet onions is in the air.

Kay Barker is making chutney with plump green tomatoes and some people still put up their own relishes and pickles, following the heritage of waste not, want not. There are dozens of commercial ones which are excellent but there is an added savor to one's own labor!

The roadsides are thick with goldenrod, and the Cape variety is bushier than that inland and more of a brownish yellow. It has a closer, thicker texture. The gardens are burnished with zinnias, bigger and brighter than inland and there are always a few late roses up to the time of killing frost.

Summer lingers in the trees but somehow there is a faint brush of color beginning, and by the end of the month the swamp maple announces the advent of true autumn. The first one I see is down by Charlie Moore's pond and I always wonder whether the burning bush in the Bible was that color.

On rainy days the rain may fall in a dense curtain, turning the world to a special twilight. Rain is not, I may say, as welcome as during the long dry spells in summer when gardens collapse. The Cape soil is so light and sandy that even a three-inch rainfall can vanish in no time. Now after a hard rain, the beach grasses have a pinky glow. (It would take years to study all the varieties of grasses in the narrow land and even these climbing my slope are infinitely varied.)

I always watch that slope when it rains so I can see the delicate colors awake. The seaweed in drifts along the water's edge begins to shine like amber when it is wet. And then of course my drab beige lawn is suddenly greening once more and will need mowing in another day!

The fog comes in any season, mysterious and sudden. The theory is that Chatham has more fog than any other part of the Cape—Chatham is the next town up-Cape. Millie and Ed have a friend who lives there and works at Nickerson's. They have told him he must keep his fog machine going a lot.

"Yesterday was clear," he said one day. "I told my wife to keep that damn machine going but she went off and forgot!"

The Cape humor, as I have observed it, involves a natural instinctive way of looking at life, and seldom involves telling amusing stories. It is a Cape Codder who will say after a snowstorm, "Wall, I haven't got around to mowing it yet!"

Or when the electricity goes out, there is a dry comment, "The boys in Boston like to take some time off."

And when the house across Mill Pond burned to the ground, Ed's comment was, "I see that nonflammable roof really is. Just as good as new—but nothing to put it on."

Their attitude toward weather never weakens. In the midst of a hurricane, I am always told, "It won't last long."

When it snows, they say, "Be all gone by morning. Won't stay on the ground."

And when day after day the Cape staggers with drought, the saying is, "It will rain soon as the wind changes 'round."

Usually they are right on every count, since the weather changes here with such remarkable rapidity.

The true descendants of the early fishermen need no weather bulletins. They have them built in their bones in some strange way, like Harry Hunt, whom I have spoken of. I don't remember any of the mid-westerners where I grew up who ever had this special weather sense. A few of the farmers

I know in Connecticut can tell by the way leaves look what is coming, but the farms are being sold off in that area for developments and this will soon be a lost art.

My friend Willie still raises a good many crops in Southbury and I can always find out from him when I am there whether it will rain or snow or freeze or thaw. I am sure the early settlers on the Cape learned their weather wisdom from the Indians.

When I think of the drama on the Cape, the first thing I remember is the day the Englishmen began their historic row from Orleans to England. They started from the beach directly across Mill Pond from my house, so a good many of my friends came over to watch the launching. The police had cordoned off the opposite area and from my windows there looked to be a lot of them. They had been watching the craft all night, since it was already loaded with gear.

So my first emotion was of sympathy for the troopers who had this extra task piled on their already burdened shoulders.

All historic occasions are confused; this was no exception. Originally they were to embark from Chatham. When they brought the craft to Mill Pond, I wondered why they were adding extra distance to their row, since the inlet from Mill Pond to the big water is quite a piece. Nobody knew why —it had to do with tides or its being easier to launch in still water. I doubt whether it was to give me a ringside view.

Rumor had it that the rowers didn't seem to be overly seasoned as to details. Some Chatham true salt-water men advised about the oars and helped with various details. At first we heard there were six men and then eight. None of us knew whether it was a dory or not. But we all agreed it was too small to cross the Atlantic! There were two men only.

They were Chay Blyth and John Ridgway. The twenty-foot open boat was called *Rose III*. They set out June 4th,

1966, at 5:30 in the afternoon. The voyage was to take them
ninety-two days, and certainly all the gods of the sea must
have been with them. Of course they wrote a book afterward
(all adventurers do) and dedicated it to the Cape Cod dory-
men who gave them a fighting chance.

It appears that from the length of oars to the stowing of
provisions, the Cape seamen were responsible for their having
that chance.

Just why they set out so late in the day has been variously
explained as to tides—but there are two tides a day—the
wind direction, and so on. But it would seem to this observer
that it would be nice to get a start by daylight on such a
trip.

But there they were on that late afternoon, stowing their
supplies in the *Rose III.*

"Why would they do a crazy thing like that?" asked someone, adjusting the binoculars.

"Just want to be first in something," said another.

"They can't possibly make it," said a third, snapping color
shots.

"There ought to be a law," said one of the men.

On the Cape, this is apt to be our final conclusion, but it always loses its force when someone points out how few laws
anyone pays any attention to.

Finally the diminished figures began to climb into the small
craft and very slowly it headed toward the inlet. Even
though these seafarers had more courage than sense, I felt a
prick of tears, and sent a prayer with them. Nobody was of-
fering to bet on their success, especially the hardy fishermen
who spent their lives battling the sea.

It turned out that after they reached the end of the inlet,
and the last point of land, there was another farewell with
more well-wishers and a flag flying. And then it grew dark,
for their take-off had been delayed, as such things always are.

They had managed not to lose the tide, which was the main thing.

So off they went and incredibly they made it, adding a footnote to history proving only that man *can* row across the Atlantic if he is lucky.

The Pilgrims had a more basic purpose, although they mislaid it after they became established. They were following a dream of religious freedom and independence. They were lucky, too, for they weren't exactly fitted to make the voyage. And even less fitted to be pioneers.

How wild and lonely the Cape must have looked with its strange deep woods and strange birds flying. The beach in Eastham where the Pilgrims first saw Indians is called First Encounter Beach, and is still a lonesome stretch of pale sand bordered with marsh grass. There is a plaque there commemorating the historic meeting. I like to go there at dusk and imagine that encounter.

What did they think, these two alien peoples? If the Indians could have foreseen what these pale shabby men were to bring to their race, would they have killed them off while there was still time? Would they have let them all starve that first desperate winter?

Instead there is Corn Hill in Truro—and the settlers were on their way down the predatory path of history.

We are never far from history on the Cape, and I mean the beginning history of this country. Of course all of America is rich with historic memories, from Jamestown and Williamsburg to the great plains the bison roamed and the Oregon trail made its bloodied way. But I think the fact the Cape is such a narrow stretch of land and is separated from the mainland makes the past more intimate. All I have learned has come in casual conversation, not in dusty research, and this gives it an immediacy.

For sixteen men under Miles Standish went exploring and
followed an Indian trail (with muskets ready). They found
the remains of a harvested cornfield, grape and strawberry
vines, and what seemed to be an Indian graveyard. At the top
of a glacial hill they came on an area of freshly dug ground.
Thirteen of the brave men stood with muskets ready while
three dug down and uncovered the Indians' cache of corn
—thirty-six fine ears—around four bushels in a woven
basket. They took it all, stuffing extras in their pockets.

Being our forefathers, they talked about it. Someday they
would repay the Indians, therefore they were not truly stealing! But they left none for the men who had planted, tended,
harvested and stored it.

I am told this corn was some yellow, some red, some mixed
with blue, and this reminds me of the special corn we planted
at Stillmeadow which was streaked with dark blue. It was the
sweetest we ever ate. I think we called it Mexican corn in
those days.

On the way back to the waiting shallop, the men came on
a sapling forming an archway over the trail. William Bradford strolled under it, whereupon the sapling sprang in air
and he hung dangling by one leg. I like to think the deer trap
was some small revenge for the Indians.

Corn Hill is a favorite spot for visitors, partly for the elegant view it gives but partly because there is still a strange-
ness about standing on the very hill where Standish once
stood.

Although the Pilgrims first landed at Provincetown, they
eventually founded the settlement at Plymouth (Plimouth
Plantation, it was called) as the harbor was better there and
there was plenty of fresh water available. By this time so
many had died of scurvy (salt meat and biscuits and beer were
staples of the diet) that most men would have set sail for the
shores of home.

They faced the prospect of clearing land, building shelters, finding food, coping with the Indians, and what they called the General Sickness which followed shortly. Most of the women had died and with them the babies they had borne in the stinking hold of the *Mayflower*. The strongest man might suddenly fall dead, and no amount of bleeding seemed to cure anyone.

But by January 14, the common house in Plimouth was roofed, although they still lived on the *Mayflower* for the most part. A few workmen stayed on shore and William Bradford was in the common house, being ill. The 14th was Sunday so, as usual, they took the day off for prayer and meditating. All during the first desperate time, they never failed to stop everything on Sunday, which is curious to reflect on, for they lost a number of much-needed work days, but this very stubbornness was probably one reason they survived at all!

They were not exactly shot with luck, for that night the common house caught fire from a spark landing on the thatch of the roof. Along with poor Bradford, the building was full of barrels of gunpowder and loaded muskets. Somehow they got him out and quenched the fire before the whole works blew up.

By February a few small houses were up, but in that month seventeen more died and were buried in unmarked graves so that the Indians would not know how few of the invaders remained. They knew the Indians watched and any man foolish enough to leave his axe in the woods never found it again. But there was no attack and somehow work went on, although by March 21 thirteen out of the eighteen wives remaining were buried on the hill.

But fortune took a turn at last when a handsome Indian brave suddenly appeared, walked right to the common house and, while they stared dumbly, raised his hand and said, "Welcome!"

This is one of the strangest parts of the whole incredible story. Samoset had known some English fishermen who had sailed this way in the past. Fortunately the fishermen had treated him better than the Pilgrims might have at first encounter. He was what might be called a travelin' man and had come down from his native Maine.

The colonists had sense enough to entertain him and put him up for the night at Stephen Hopkins' house, but they stationed a guard outside all night with instructions to fire if the guest made a move. The next day Samoset left and came back with five more braves who were entertained and then "sang and danced" and agreed to trade with the Pilgrims, swapping deer and beaver skins for tools.

The next time Samoset returned, he brought a priceless gift in the person of a Patuxet brave named Tisquantum, later to go down in history as Squanto. Bradford called him a special instrument of God for their good, as indeed he was. His first act was to catch an armload of eels which gave the colonists' diet a real lift.

He taught them to fertilize the corn hills with dead fish and showed them how to catch the alewives in mid-April that swarmed up Town River. He helped plant three to each hill with the heads closest to the kernels. And exactly five kernels to a hill.

During the early starvation days, the Englishmen had managed to shoot some wild ducks and geese, but as fishermen they had managed nothing much but a cod. It seems strange to think they came to this wilderness with so few skills for survival. Even the barley and oats they planted died and without the Indian corn the colony would never have survived.

With Samoset and Squanto's help, a truce was signed with the Indians which included the provision that when the Indians came to the colony they should leave bows and arrows behind, and when the white men went to Indian places they would leave their muskets behind. Such a wise rule may have prevented a good deal of trigger- and arrow-happy men. It is too bad nations today don't follow such an agreement.

By mid-September the school busses rumble along and yards seem empty without the bevies of small children. The dogs wander around waiting for school to be over and they definitely look bored. But mothers, I notice, are not idle. They are cleaning house, airing the woolens, sunning blankets, painting lawn furniture.

I know this is going on in Appleton, Wisconsin, and Freeport, Illinois, and all over the country. It proves, I think, that women operate with the same general rhythm and it follows the seasons as naturally as dark follows day.

This is a planning time for them. For now there is time enough to see how shabby the living-room wallpaper is and in what terrible shape the kitchen floor is after a summer of sandy feet walking on it. I always feel like shopping for something new, almost anything, and Millie and I spend some afternoons in the furniture and department stores, not to mention Snow's.

Then comes the day when Millie decides to look at my last winter's clothes. This is always a minor disaster, for they all look absolutely impossible. Some are now too big, some too long, some have rusty zippers, some are way out of style and some, as Millie says, just don't do anything for me.

I tell her I cannot afford to wear anything that doesn't, for I need all the help I can get, not being glamorous at best.

Summer wear can now be moved to another closet and I

always know in my heart that the dresses I have most cherished will never be all right next June.

Men can ignore this struggle for the most part. On cool days they simply reach for a sweater. When it rains, they get out the same old storm jacket. Jimmy DeLory, the best-dressed, hangs up his soft blue gabardine jump suit and wears his gorgeous tangerine fuzzy one when he takes off what he calls his grease-monkey suit after a hard day's work. There may be men who are worried about fall wardrobes, but I have never known one.

Most of the Orleans men work in the yards on their afternoons off and until dark weekdays. It's a good time to paint screens before putting them away and to check storm windows and do the last garden chores. One of the best things about Orleans life is that most men work near enough to come home for lunch and to get home when there is still a piece of day left. Even the ones who commute to Hyannis are back for supper, and usually early enough to do a few chores outside.

Big-city life adds long extra hours for almost everyone just to get to work and then get back again. There is a place on the New Haven road in Connecticut where cars line up daily for car pools. Some go as far as the whole way into New York City, some to Bridgeport. After these workers reach the parked cars at day's end, they still have to drive to their own homes. I think of them when I ride down Tonset Road in late afternoon and see neighbors already safely parked in their own driveways.

The prevailing sentiment is that nobody can expect to make as much money staying on-Cape.

"But money isn't everything," they say in one of the truest clichés ever uttered.

The Cape does not seem to be the kind of place for big

money, except for a few retired millionaires. Neither is it a locality of massive slums or ghettos or those dreadful factory neighborhoods such as one sees going through Providence. We pass these on the way to the Cape and my heart always cracks to see a few dying geraniums in some of the tenement windows. Coming out of the smoke pall and the areas piled with rotting scrap metal, there comes a faint salty tang to the air like a message of hope for the traveler. But I keep thinking of the folk who never get away from the slums at all.

Then there is the bridge arching over the sapphire blue of the canal and the clean air blowing and the narrow land seems indeed a Heaven to dream of!

In October, the classic brilliance of autumn appears. A good many Cape dwellers choose this time to go to Maine, Vermont and New Hampshire for the spectacle. Now the radio and the newspapers announce a kind of color table, informing as to the progress of the foliage, winding up with the peak of nature's display. People try to plan just the right weekend to go and since it varies from year to year, schedules are hard to set up.

When they all get back, they compare notes as to their success and deciding whether they really got to the north at the correct time.

At this time, I realize I am an outsider, for I remember the Wisconsin woodlands from my childhood and the unbelievable beauty of the Connecticut hills near Stillmeadow. The farm itself, when the giant sugar maples turn, makes the eyes ache with scarlets and golds.

So I view the narrow land in October and find a special beauty all its own. The colors are softer and the deep blue of the sea frames them. The predominant tone is the garnet of the red oaks. Then there are the cranberry bogs, spread carpets of deep ruby. Some swamp maple and some woodbine

Sand dunes. (*John Schram*)

add a touch of flame. But the pines seem to be a reassurance of immortality and the whole Cape sings with their sturdy greens.

Then there are the beach grasses, a tide of pinky brown rising up from the shore to the slopes. From my window I see my own hillside and it is so lovely I feel dizzy just trying to identify the cinnamon shades, sand-beige, faint purples.

The seaweed itself, in drifts at the water's edge, turns so dark as to be almost black. Perhaps this is why the sand of the beach glitters with an extra silver-gilt sheen. At very low tide, the charcoal mudflats appear, rich and primal.

Here and there pale gold honeysuckle blooms as if summer were beginning again and occasional roses open in the blue air. I probably do not make friends when I ask my usual question.

"Why should you go to Maine or New Hampshire or Vermont? What could ever be as beautiful as Cape Cod in autumn?"

Since the killing frost comes late, some gardens are bright and everywhere you ride along winding roads the rose haws of the wild roses stitch the landscape with bright red tinged with orange.

The salt ponds, which are countless, have a special sapphire color as they drink the brilliant blue of the autumn sky and most of them are bordered with wild berry-bearing bushes. The wild blackberry canes turn a deep purple misted over with silver. Pokeberry bushes have their inky-black berries, and the birds at Still Cove gather them and drop them on the split-rail fence. They stain the wood like dye. (I seem to remember the juice was used as a dye in early days but that the berries are poison to people.)

The Full Hunter's Moon makes October nights luminous. It is the color of antique gold and the stars jewel the clear sky. People drive to Nauset or Rock Harbor to store up the

glory against the gray days ahead. For November comes too
soon!

One major topic of conversation concerns Daylight Saving
being over. I have never heard a single soul speak a good
word for setting the clock back an hour. Nobody I know in
Connecticut likes it either. Some of us only set one or two
clocks back and keep on with our familiar schedule for a
while, but in the end we give in.

Nature, however, sets her own time schedule. She decides
when the first white frost will come and when the geese go
over and when the leaves will begin to drift down and when
the hibernating small animals will feel the urge to snug down
in their burrows. She brings the first heavy storms and turns
the air to brittle cold.

And, clocks or no, man follows her plan. Fire on the open
hearth, storm windows, warm boots, furnaces clean, bird
feeders ready—these mark nature's timetable. The richness
of October ends too soon, and it is time to stop admiring the
landscape and get ready to cope with another season!

Although the Cape seems to be such a separate entity, the
events of our times affect it. One of the most incredible was
what they called the Cuban Incident. It happened in March
1970, but we were still talking of it in October. My information came from the accounts in the local newspapers, the
radio, and of course conversations with Cape Codders. Some
of the stories conflicted, but here is what I gathered took
place.

The *Jocelyn C*, a sixty-foot fishing vessel out of Chatham,
was steaming through the Bahamian Channel after a rough
time with head winds. She carried a good deal of electronic
equipment to be used for hunting sixteenth-century buried
treasure, and was bound for Caribbean waters in the vicinity
of Jamaica, where treasure ships are thought to have sunk.

Captain Sten Carlson said it was the best-equipped fishing boat ever to sail on such a hunt. I may say, to native Cape Codders this seems like a perfectly sensible project for a Cape fishing boat! Another purpose was said to be to test the oceanographic equipment.

Off the lower Bahamas, near Cay Lobos, a Cuban gunboat suddenly appeared alongside, closing fast as Captain Carlson said. It signaled the *Jocelyn C* to stop, but Captain Carlson steamed on, edging to the north.

Finally a Cuban officer shouted, "Do you want to go to Cuba?"

"No, *absolutamente*," said Carlson.

He was ordered to follow the gunboat, but he kept the *Jocelyn C* edging to the north until the Cubans lowered their guns and sent a boarding party. Carlson and Crockett, the second in command, treated the invaders with food and drink and tales of the wonders of Cape Cod until one had to be put to bed "not feeling well."

Around midnight they reached a big harbor on Cuba's north shore alongside a sunken cement ship (like the target ship in Cape Cod Bay, said Carlson). They were lined up and interviewed and then escorted in to Caibarien where breakfast was served in a sometime villa. At 3:00 A.M., after they had enjoyed beer, a fifteen-pound tin of biscuits, canned peaches, cigars and coffee a photographer took their pictures with an old Polaroid.

At 7:00 A.M. another breakfast was served, including eggs, and for lunch there was red snapper and beer. Then the Cuban captain boarded the *Jocelyn C* to examine the vessel, where he enjoyed gin and tonics. Suddenly there was a telephone call and word came the Americans must leave Cuba immediately. By that time it was growing dark and a stiff wind blew and Captain Carlson said if they could not wait until morning they would need some fuel.

When he explained he needed 800 gallons of diesel, the Cubans nearly fainted but finally managed 450 gallons. This had to be loaded in 55-gallon drums but eventually, with long cordial farewells, the Cape Codders were under way for Jamaica.

Naturally Mrs. Carlson was interviewed at the home in Orleans, very pretty and very composed as a sailor's wife should be. She said she did not know anything about C.I.A. agents; her husband was treasure hunting. The State Department had previously denied that the boat was on a U. S. government mission.

Cape Cod is pretty proud of the *Jocelyn C* and her crew who managed by their good sense and humor to make what might have been an ugly affair into a rather gay encounter.

Perhaps this is another Cape Cod legend—a new one.

As I write, Indian Summer and the Full Beaver Moon are scheduled. In mid-month, Indian Summer is a special blessing, for November is a chancy time on Cape Cod. Heavy rains gray the skies often, the wind blows hard, fog rolls in over the dunes. The tempo of life slows down and furnaces begin to gobble up oil. The alewives go back to sea from the herring runs, and the summer bird songs are gone.

But Indian Summer brings gold-and-blue weather, warm enough to walk the beaches and sit in the sun and do a few extra outside chores. The leaves are fallen, except for the oaks, and last raking is in order. Most people save the leaves for compost but a few burn them. There is nothing sweeter than the scent of burning leaves as the blue smoke drifts into the still air, but nothing makes us conservationists angrier.

With all the struggle against air pollution, there are still those who pay no attention. They destroy the nourishment in the leaves, which nature needs in her cycle, and one man I have seen has a fire that clouds his whole neighborhood.

Indoors, gardeners now begin to turn to African violets, geraniums and gloxinias. The gloxinia is a lush tropical-looking plant with enormous velvety blossoms shading from deep cream to rosy red, the leaves are big as cabbage leaves and a very dark green. I somehow feel like apologizing to mine for being in a northern clime!

Millie and I have tried wintering geraniums over but without success. Experts have advised us but we still failed. The two tubs by the wing door bloomed madly all summer and they were the new brilliant coral color so lovely against gray shingles. But we just put the tubs down cellar after the first big frost.

African violets are most satisfying, spreading small bouquets of purple and rose and ivory in their pots. If they are fed weekly with regular African violet food, they do not ask for anything more except to be talked to daily.

The nicest house geranium I know is at Barbara Lovely's in a bracket hanging on the wall above the dropleaf breakfast table, and it makes me wonder why more of us do not keep house plants on window walls.

I have been recommending this to my friends but have yet to acquire the bracket myself! I manage begonias on the kitchen windowsill and they are gay and hardy. But when I hear Thalassa Cruso, the plant lady, discuss house plants on TV, I realize my limitations, for she seems to turn a whole house into a bower.

My friend Eileen DeLory makes beautiful bouquets of tall grasses and seed pods and cattails and so does my neighbor Kay. I settle for the beach lavender which grows along my beach and keeps its soft pink-lilac color all winter. I have never seen it anywhere except on the Cape and I do not know the botanical name for it. We call it beach or sea lavender.

Pine branches bring color into the house and the pine cones are decorative. And so even the gray days are not so bad, although I admit they can be depressing.

On one such day the wind blew with gale force but I went out and drove to my favorite Rock Harbor to get a change from the house. It had rained hard but a break in the clouds brought a faint glow to sky and sea. The bay was crested with white and the air filled with the sound of the wind.

Then I saw, way out, a very small fishing boat heading away from land. It vanished in the waves, then rose, vanished again and every time it sank out of sight I expected it would never reappear.

I felt like racing over the dark sand to call to the skipper to turn back to safety. I had never seen anything so frightening as this tiny craft swallowed by the great waves. But the boat kept heading out—and heading out—and finally was so far into the vast of the bay that I could hardly make out the prow as it rose and sank with the impact of the sea.

I sat for a long time thinking about the courage of the men aboard her—were there two or three? Probably only two, since she was so small. How did they come to be so fearless? They were dipping into the horizon by now, and the only other craft visible was the venerable lightship that rides forever on the sandbar, tenanted only by gulls and barnacles.

Cape Cod fishermen have been intimate with wind and weather for generations and I reassured myself that these would make it back to port when they were through with their business. And as I started the motor and slid through the puddles on the landing, I said a prayer for them.

They had given me a special gift on that dark and bitter day, for I was preoccupied with problems and anxieties and the sight of that valiant fishing boat made me feel inspired to plunge head on into my own high seas of life. Not to turn back, to seek an easy shore, to abandon the day's journeying. And if that small craft rode the stormy waves, why should I feel swamped by unimportant crises?

On the way home to Mill Pond, the sun shone, the bare branches of the elms glittered, the old white houses had a polished look. I began my customary off-key singing, "Oh beautiful Cape Cod—oh beautiful Cape Cod!"

Perhaps we all need such a waking from the anxieties of this troubled and terrible era, a small viewing of the true spirit of man!

One asset the Cape has in abundance is dogs. When you see a small boy running down a road, you look for the dog pounding along behind. As you drive to town, nearly every yard is properly furnished by a dog. The dogs come in all sizes and shapes, but there are more mixtures than thoroughbreds. On our side of Tonset, we note how many part-Labrador retrievers there are, and the reason for this lies dozing on Orin Tovrov's lawn. For Smoky has fathered a good many puppies, and since he is a fine gentleman, most of the offspring are sleek ebony tail-waggers. One or two take after the mother, obviously, and chase cars, but we all watch for them.

Holly, my champion Irish, was the best friend of most of Tonset and dropped in to call on her regular rounds. The rest of the time she skimmed along the beach of Mill Pond or swam halfway across it. She invariably brought me a present of a very dead fish just as I was leaving for a dress-up party. By the time I extricated the fish and stashed it in the trash can, I smelled of fish rather than Mary Chess White Lilac.

One fatal day she lugged up a decaying fish as large as her whole front and my departure for that party was delayed while I threw up while trying to embed the skeleton in an old towel. Holly was discouraged, but patient. This was the most elegant present she had ever brought and she felt my praise was lukewarm at best!

The Stillmeadow cockers and Irish were obedience-trained as well as being shown in breed if they were outstanding. By the time two cockers, Linda and Sister, and Holly the Irish began to come to the Cape, they had graduated. We had many memories of plodding around in broiling sun or heavy snow with the current trainee idling along on the leash. It was hard work, no mistake about it, but as we looked back, we felt a deep nostalgia. The silver trophies and blue ribbons meant more to us than any slab-sized diamond could mean to Elizabeth Taylor.

So I was especially pleased to visit the dog-training class in Chatham this past spring. I went with a neighbor, Myra, and her charming unreconstructed Cricket. Cricket is about the size of a small Irish and has a tawny coat, but it is anybody's guess as to her primary origins. She was an abandoned orphan when the Morrisons took her in and gave her a home.

It was a cold night, and fog lay heavy over Chatham. Seventeen dogs with their handlers were sloshing toward the gymnasium and finally gathered inside. The trainer, a pencil-slim young man, lined the class up. He looked as if he might be a long-distance runner and I reflected this would go well with dog training. He had the patent-leather hair which does look so much better than shaggy curls scraping the shoulders, and he wore slacks and a jersey without a psychedelic note in them.

The class had been running eight weeks and most of the dogs heeled well, sat on command, and the advanced ones *stayed* while the owners walked away.

"Forward—about   turn—left   turn—right   turn—" the trainer gave the commands in an easy voice. "Down your dog—"

This was a good idea, according to the St. Bernard. He flattened his bulk out happily and then refused to stand up again. A St. Bernard is about as easy to lift up as a ten-ton truck. The miniature poodles were no problem and the collies flopped easily. There were ten or eleven identifiable breeds; the rest were mixed.

During a break, the star of the class came to the center of the floor. A seven-and-a-half-year-old girl named Cindy had been to the last dog show with her Sheltie and won in breed as well as making the qualifying score of 147 in Novice A.

"And if you ask me who my sweetheart is," said the trainer, "I can tell you she is standing right here!"

Cindy blushed and looked fondly at her dog.

After about two hours, the class broke up with the final instructions ringing in their ears.

"Don't stop working your dog. Find time every day— even a few minutes. Don't let either of you forget all you have learned. I'll be seeing you at the shows."

A number of them would undoubtedly be at the next Cape Cod show and I wished them well. I was certain nothing would ever stop Cindy, for she had that quality spelling success.

"I hope when she grows up she can spend her life with dogs all around her," I said as we drove back to Orleans.

Cricket, in the back seat, sighed. The excitement had worn her out. She would have said, had I asked, that the one exercise she would never put up with was being left alone while her owner walked away!

This was always the most difficult exercise for the cockers, too. Sister would plump herself down as docile as a dove but by the time I had moved five steps away, a small patter of paws came after me. When she finally got her Utility degree, my friends said they never expected me to live through it.

Aside from heeling easily on leash, I believe the most valuable exercise of all the many there are is the drop on command of a lifted arm. This can save a dog's life in case he starts across the road and a speeding car appears. It is also very handy when a skunk is encountered, as I found out.

But the obedience work was well designed in the beginning for it has nothing to do with tricks. It has to do with practical living and often the owner learns as much as the dog.

I was happy to know that along with sailing, water-skiing, surfboarding, golf and tennis, the Cape offered something as important as classes for obedience.

Today I took Amber to Eastham to Dr. Schneider's Veterinary Hospital. We had been talking it over for a week and putting it off. An Abyssinian has very small delicate paws, so limber that she can stand on tiptoe in a way no cat I ever knew could. But since she cannot run free and thrash around in the woods, her claws grow too long and must be manicured. I have one friend who can do her own cat's clipping, but I think an expert is usually advisable, since if you clip the least bit too far inward, you damage the kitty. The line where the blood supply stops and the minute nails should be trimmed is a very fine one.

Amber is resigned to her carrying case but extremely hostile to being trimmed. Kim Schneider's hospital is a very old Cape house set back in the midst of lilacs and in autumn the flagstone path has the last of the fallen leaves on it. The yard looks so serene that it is hard to imagine the line of desperate owners who traverse that path with their sick pets. But in any season it is hard to find a place to park a car.

I settled for having Fred Southworth, the big amiable assistant, lug Amber in. He still grieves over the loss of his dog, killed by a hit-and-run driver, but is always encouraging to patients' owners. The patients, I noticed, vary from pedigreed elegance to back-alley refugees, but the owners all LOOK ALIKE. They look scared.

Kim is a slim young doctor, deft and quiet, expert in diagnosis and treatment. He has those shining dark eyes one could drown in. I have known only a few with this special quality.

"Well, Amberino," he said, "let's just take care of you."

Even the most besotted owner could not admire Amber's behavior. Screaming and struggling and hissing, she took both of us to hold her.

"She's pulling out your sweater," said Kim, as he clipped one recalcitrant paw.

"My best Beth Bishop one," I said.

Now Amber knows very well this is a regular process and takes very little time. But she will never give in. And, in my experience, this is one difference between a dog and a cat. Usually a dog will accept whatever you dish out once the idea permeates. But a cat feels violated in a strange way by any treatment. And Amber thinks she owes it to herself to battle to the end, to the last hind paw, even though she knows very well exactly what is going on and that it is a minor matter.

Curiously enough, when we get home, she skims through the house with great delight. She does not really like her claws to get so long they curve inward, and if she is overdue for a visit to Kim she works away herself trying to trim them. So it is just the principle of the thing that she fights for.

By the time we came out today, the office was jammed with wriggling puppies, tongue-lolling hunting dogs, and one leaden-eyed cat, too ill to complain. Amber lunged around in her carrying case until the door closed behind us, whereupon she flattened herself comfortably and began to wash herself.

Orleans, with so many advantages, is especially blessed to have a fine veterinarian. We used to have to go all the way to Hyannis to the topnotch Dr. Bernstein, and I still remember a nightmare trip with my Irish hemorrhaging on the back seat of the car. Doctor B. saved her life, but that trip was

Amber at Still Cove. (*John Schram, Cape Cod Photos*)

about like trying to bicycle to Alaska as far as I was concerned.

One quality a great veterinarian has (which our Dr. Whitney in New Haven demonstrated to us long ago) is empathy with the owners. I often think the owner needs more treatment than the animal. There is a sound reason for this, of course. A human patient can describe a pain, even a baby can yell a lot of information, but a dog or cat is helpless. Most owners are frantic trying to diagnose the problem themselves, and by the time the patient is on the examining table, they have imagined a thousand fatal ailments.

"Well, I don't think we have to worry about this too much," says Kim. And the words fall like manna.

The Indians had dogs, and so did the Pilgrims, but not much is ever said as to what they were like. The spaniel was a very early breed in England and I seem to remember one Pilgrim did have a spaniel, but it would be interesting to know the derivation of the Indians' dogs. They must have been hunters, and presumably native to this country. I have never read about cats—although cats go back four thousand years to the time when Amber's forebears were deified in Egypt.

But when I think about that first settlement in this wild land, I always imagine a dog or so, for dogs and man belong together. Perhaps a few bones from the first Thanksgiving were shared with somebody's dog!

The first Thanksgiving was proclaimed by the new young Governor Bradford. By then the settlement had twenty acres of corn and the Pilgrims were getting along with the nearby Indians and fish were plentiful and houses were roofed. The idea of a harvest festival was not new, for as far back as history goes men have celebrated them, usually with the idea of appeasing their gods.

Massasoit, the Indian chief, was invited to this feast, and turned up with ninety men! Fortunately the Indians added five deer to the provisions to help out. The Pilgrims had wild turkeys, lobsters, eels and other fish. Also they by now had parsnips, turnips, onions, carrots. They had wine from the wild grapes, and one expert says it was spiced with gin, but I do not see how they had any gin to spare by this time. The corn came into its own, in ashcakes, hoecakes and roasted. It is said Squanto made Indian pudding of molasses and corn-meal cooked in a bag.

Only ten women had survived the struggle to establish the settlement, but the men turned the spits as the fowl and meat roasted, and all in all, it was a very happy holiday feast.

Legend has it that some of the settlers still wished they had decided to settle on Cape Cod, which would have probably been Wellfleet where the harbor was an inviting one. But there was a better supply of fresh water in Plymouth and most of them thought the soil was better. It was a wise deci-sion as far as our time is concerned for there is more room for expansion in "America's Home Town" on the mainland than there would have been at Wellfleet.

I still remember the day of one of the various celebrations when a replica of the *Mayflower* sailed into Provincetown harbor before continuing to a big fanfare at Plymouth across the bay. A bitter cold rain was falling and fog lay over the narrow land as Jill, my partner at Stillmeadow, drove me down the narrow slice of street to a restaurant at the water's edge. The miserable weather had driven more people inside than there was room for and the poor waitresses were rushing about in a state of panic.

In a dispirited silence, customers spooned lukewarm chow-der or wrestled with cold lobsters. Then someone cried, "There she comes!" The place buzzed into life as we all jammed against the windows. Jill had binoculars and passed

them around and it was a half-hour later when a pretty Portuguese waitress got them back to us.

There she was, dreamlike in the gray air, a tall ship with
chopped-off squarish bow. We could see flags flying and the
faint outlines of the cutters escorting her. The sea was running high and progress was slow but the *Mayflower* finally
made it and dropped anchor.

I thought the weather could not have been more fitting, for
the whole voyage and landing of the original ship had been
beset by the worst weather possible in New England (partly
because they sailed the wrong time of year). But I could
imagine how the wild lonely shore looked to the Pilgrims
when it first rose like a shadow against the desolate sky. They
were here, in the new land, the land of hope and dreams and
promise. "Land Ho" was a beginning!

No one ever directs you to Corn Hill without relating the
whole series of events. A Cape Codder tells you to turn left
for First Encounter Beach and adds that is where the Pilgrims
met and fought the Indians. Or, if you go down Snow Shore
Road and meet a man walking the beach, you will hear about
the French Cable that had a housing right there, just a short
ways down. It was the first cable between France and the
United States.

And you can find where the British soldiers were buried
during the War of 1812 if you ask a native. Never a week
passes without my learning something more about the long-
ago.

"Oh, that house is full of ghosts," I hear. "British seamen
died of the plague there. Seems they still try to go home."

"A witch lived down the road—well that's what they
say. Not that anybody believes in witches. It's what they
say."

I like the sense of the past, perhaps because the world is in such a troubled state at the present. I like to think this country survived the beginnings, the Civil War, the subsequent wars and may yet survive the age of atom bombs, although so many experts predict the end of this planet within a short range of time. There has always been an inner core of strength in this conglomerate nation and in such a place as Cape Cod it is easy to have faith in it.

The infinite variety in the aspect of the Cape makes it impossible to describe and imperative that one keeps trying! From hour to hour the sea and land change. I had thought all of the times I have written down words about sunrise had really covered the subject for good.

So yesterday I got up at four-fifteen to turn up the thermostat, for the house was so cold, I had waked up. I went into the living room where Amber was buried in the elegant wool throw Faith Baldwin gave me. Only a satiny-seal-dark paw was visible, for she had wound herself into a ball.

I looked out of the picture window toward Nauset, and gave up all thoughts of sleep. The bit of the big water I could see was midnight blue. Above, the long sweep of sky kindled the horizon. Below my house, Mill Pond looked as if it had been polished to a silver sheen. But all of the shore was still ebony, all around Mill Pond and all along the inlet leading to Nauset and on Nauset Heights itself. Nobody, I thought, would believe this—water and sky alight and all land-mass black.

Then I saw with wonder that the low pines and bayberry bushes and shrubs on the eastern edge of Mill Pond were reflected in the stillness of the water, distinctly visible. It appeared they were growing up from Mill Pond, rooted deep below in the sea-bottom, and reaching toward the sky, although upside down! The separate branches seemed to have a lacy texture. An artist would have outlined them in charcoal —or perhaps he would have simply cut his throat!

At five, I started back to bed because I was fevered with so much wonder. And then from my bedroom window, I got no ease, for over the small duck pond came the drifting veil of morning fog, rolling against the wooded shore in a silent surf.

So Amber yawned herself awake and came to perch on the narrow windowsill and suggest if it were really time to get up, howabouta dish of minced flounder?

One of the busiest places in Orleans around Thanksgiving time is Mayo's Duck Farm. The big farm itself has been sold for building lots, and the buildings where the housing and processing were carried on were burned down. This caused a major disturbance on the part of everyone who saw the pillars of smoke rising and felt sure a bomb had gone off. The police and fire department telephones were swamped.

Now all that is left is Mrs. Mayo's food center, on the road to Nauset. I don't know how to define it in any other term. In season, there is what is called the Quackery, where visitors eat outdoors, carrying their paper plates of hamburgers, hotdogs, steaks or whatever from the open-air grill counter. In the main building there are frozen casseroles, clam pies, chicken pies, canapés. Homemade bread, rolls, pies and cakes, cookies and tarts are on sale. There are also sandwiches, lobster and tuna rolls, containers of potato salad and cole slaw.

Weekends, chicken and ducklings turn on electric spits. And at Thanksgiving time, Mrs. Mayo takes orders for the turkey dinner and half the town lines up for crisp crackling turkeys, smelling of herbs and onions. One may also order the "fixin's"—cranberry sauce, squash, turnips.

Now when families arrive for the holiday, the lady of the

house does not have to spend all of her time basting the turkey and baking the mince or apple pies. Mrs. Mayo's turkeys are delicious and if you drive past on the way to the great beach, the air is rich with the savory smells.

Women who really love to wrestle with the biggest feast of the year still may get uncooked turkeys and make their own oyster stuffing or whatever. Some favor crumbled corn bread or chestnuts added. Then there is always conversation about the best way to roast the holiday bird. Some advocate wrapping it in buttered brown paper. Some roast it overnight at 200°. Some like it put in at 400° to brown and then roasted slowly for hours.

But one turkey will go down in history as Eileen's turkey.

Eileen and Jimmy DeLory live in one of the most charming houses in Orleans, tucked in the piney woods on the edge of a salt-water pond. They are known for their warm hospitality and Eileen is one of those who must be called a gourmet cook. In every sense of the word.

This particular Thanksgiving, the house was to be full of guests, as usual, and Eileen had a magnificent turkey stuffed and seasoned. She put it in the oven when they went to bed for the long slow cooking to bring out the flavor. In the morning when she got up, she went to turn the oven higher. Through the open oven door she viewed her masterpiece, resting in the roasting pan. It had rested all night for the oven was cold as a winter stone!

She turned the oven up high and began to wonder how long dinner could be delayed.

"Never mind," said Jimmy. "We'll just sit around and have an extra drink."

The oven began to work, then thought better of it.

Eventually the electrician was located and the oven fixed.

"That turkey took seventeen hours to get done," said Eileen.

We all agreed there was a lot to be said for the old cast-iron cookstove! I remembered getting up in the night at Stillmeadow to throw more wood in ours, but there was just nothing about it to get out of order. True, it had no self-cleaning oven and when that oven got rusty it was a deadly job to clean it. However, I think of it with nostalgia as I turn the switch on my wonder appliance and wait to be sure the electricity hasn't gone off on the Cape because a cable has been broken somewhere this side of the bridge.

And whenever Eileen reminisces about her seventeen-hour turkey, she recalls a simpler era.

The prayers this Thanksgiving are the same as they have been for more years than we like to count. Now we pray that next Thanksgiving we may reaffirm our faith in the world as a planet where peace is more than a hazy dream. In every city and town and small village in our country during these years, the young soldiers have been coming home from foreign soil to be buried.

I think again of Stephen Spender's poem:

> Born of the sun
> They travelled a short while
> Toward the sun
> Leaving the vivid air
> Signed with their honour.

They come home to the Cape, this quiet narrow land. They are buried in the cemeteries where the sea wind always blows and the sound of the surf is their requiem. The families can tuck their letters with the strange musty smell in with the family treasures in the sea chests or old desks. They can save the Cape paper with the photograph and obit of the boy.

And then they can walk the shining beaches and stare at the vast of the ocean and lick the salt spray from their lips as the salt tears fall. And next Memorial Day there will be more flowers by that newly carved gravestone.

November rains fall with a driving power and the level of the ponds rises. The cranberry bogs are flooded when the frost warnings come from the mainland weather stations. The leaves come down with the rain and the shape of trees comes plain to the eye without the cloak of color. When the sun comes out, the branches look polished. Rock Harbor is no longer so busy with boats and is very still as the sun drops her golden ball. The evening air has a touch of winter to come.

Winter

OLD HOUSES, CHATHAM

Yesterday's houses under winter sun
Stood blank-eyed beside an empty sea
For summer folk go when summer's done
Leaving the houses and the sapphire sea.

Once long ago men walked the terraces
(Before my first reluctant breath).
Women in pale silks and laces
Stepped gentle on the scissored heath.

The houses deeply porticoed
Are broad of window, columned well.
Today they face a silent road
And that is all there is to tell.

Yesterday's summers come no more.
Only the tides invade the shore.

The Full Cold Moon rises over Mill Pond with the peculiar polished look a winter moon has. No other moon has the look of a winter moon, for it is almost ice-white. The water below also seems polished, smooth ebony. The stillness crackles with the chill.

Winter on the narrow land is the most controversial subject there is. When I am inland, at Stillmeadow, friends call from Orleans to sympathize with me for not being in the Florida of New England. Some of them say cold rains fall but the temperature is moderate. But some of them describe the Cape as an extension of the North Pole.

No amount of personal research on my part has made me feel qualified to state exactly what a Cape winter is like. I can only assemble the various reports and add my own experience when I am here. Then I compare it with my Connecticut valley, which is revealing. It can be thirty below at Stillmeadow, with snow drifts five feet deep so I cannot open a single door of the house. Sometimes the mail does not get through to the box at the corner of Jeremy Swamp Road, sometimes the school bus does not run, and the radio spends all day announcing cancellations.

This is my frame of reference for winter weather and as I dial the phone for my beloved Art Olsen, the plumber, I always reflect that it takes a valorous man to plunge through

the snow at midnight to get my furnace going again before
the rest of the pipes freeze (the back kitchen always freezes at
ten below).

Now there is a curious quality most people have, certainly
I do. I feel a kind of arrogant pride because the weather is so
deadly, breaking records every few days. Think of surviving
the coldest day in the recorded history of the area! We all
check our thermometers and if the telephones are working,
exchange data on just how cold it is by the back door.

Along with this goes a lot of comparison as to which winter has been the worst in recent memory. Usually we decide
last winter was really the worst but that is partly because the
current winter is only half over and we do not know what is
coming. But, except for the January thaw, winter is all of one
piece in the valley, long and bitter and deep with snow and
with branches and electric wires cracking with ice.

Now on Cape Cod, when I am there in winter, I can understand the variety of reports I have had. For both opposing
viewpoints are correct. It is indeed the Florida of New England.

"Can't see why folks run down to Florida when it's so
good on-Cape."

But a sudden shift brings the north wind in and the sky
thickens with an ice storm. The temperature may be only fifteen degrees but that wind cuts like a knife from the deep-
freeze. You feel you could cut it in chunks and build a windy
igloo of it except that your lungs tighten up so you stagger to
the nearest shelter and wrestle the door shut if possible.

When it snows, the town reacts with disbelief. Last winter,
during a real blizzard, life stood still. The town plow
couldn't defeat it and Jimmy DeLory battled desperately
with his plow to get to beleaguered Margaret Stanger, who
claims she has the worst driveway in Orleans, and is never
disputed. This driveway lunges up a steep hill and is one-

width narrow, like my own. Moreover it leaves Monument Road in an invisible right angle.

But in my experience it is a fact that snow and ice do not last as they do inland. Cape people, so far as I know, do not lay in supplies enough to carry them indefinitely the way we do inland. And nobody prepares to budget the furnace oil or the fireplace wood.

Last winter great ice cakes piled up at Rock Harbor and along the shores to Provincetown, and all the photographers managed to photograph them, and there were pictures in the newspapers. So it was, they said, an exceptional winter.

But more often, snow and ice melt when the wind changes and the sun comes out. There has always been a theory that the Gulf current which sweeps around the Cape tempers the climate, keeping it warmer in winter, although lately I read that one expert has decided the Gulf current has nothing to do with the Cape weather at all.

Some people believe that the fact that the Cape is such a narrow arm extending into the vastness of the sea is the main factor in Cape weather. I am inclined to go along with them. For certainly the expanse of water surrounding the land is one reason for the coolness of summer.

I think, compared to Connecticut, winters on Cape Cod are mild, with plenty of raw sea-borne winds and driving rains but not anywhere near the Arctic eternity of December, January, February, March inland.

However, weather is such a personal emotion that I will never argue with anyone who has a different opinion. I only record my own observations and leave it to others to have theirs.

At the moment, the amount of rain impresses me, for my roof is leaking and a stream of chilly water is descending from the attic to the hall off the living room. I notice it always leaks at night when nothing can be done but put buck-

ets underneath. And wait for Dick Smith to come when the
roof has dried off.

But I know, if I reason it out, that it does not really rain so
much harder on the Cape (but it does SOME). It is just that the
roof at Stillmeadow is stouter than the roof at Still Cove.

Winter is not an easy season in New England—but
without it, where would the ecstasy of a New England
spring be?

One sad change this past year is the death of Lloyd Ellis.
He was one of those men that are never forgotten. In fact,
hardly a week goes by without someone in town speaking of
him as if he were still bouncing around in Ellis' market or
driving the truck along Main Street with careful abandon.

When I think of him, I remember not so much how good
he was to everyone but his round smiling face and constant
good cheer. When he stopped to admire my view of Mill
Pond, I saw all over again how beautiful it is.

When anyone mentions his name the final comment is that
it was good that he died on the way home from a day's fishing and this was indeed fitting.

"That's the way he would want it," we say.

By now, after almost a year of the new management at Ellis's, we are adjusted to the modernization of the store, the
new counters, the fish section, the machines doing the ac-
counting (instead of the slow pencil adding things up). The
new staff is friendly and accommodating and all the merchandise is filed according to kind. Nevertheless, it was difficult to
get used to the bill with something printed on the bottom: A
CHARGE ACCOUNT IS AN ACCOMMODATION. WE EXPECT PROMPT
PAYMENT.

"The new owner probably can't afford to carry everybody
who runs out of money when the season is bad," said Millie.

There will never be another like Lloyd Ellis.

We are no longer in the personal age and I often wonder whether the new age of efficiency can ever be as satisfying. Children now being brought up will be accustomed to being numbers instead of individuals no doubt, but I prefer to be a person instead of a row of digits!

The bird feeders and suet cages are filled all over Orleans. The winter birds are always hungry. The chickadees and nuthatches and bluejays are most common and bring life and color to the dark winter days. The bluejays on the Cape are a more vivid blue but seem a bit smaller to me. My neighbor's cardinals are in residence along with towhees. My own mockingbirds now stay all season and the gulls go over Mill Pond as usual. I suspect there is more money spent on bird food than on any other single item in the community. Some people make their own mixtures but Helen Beals puts out all sorts of leftovers and reports her birds love anything from blueberry muffins to macaroni and cheese.

I can attest to the fact that her yard is aflutter with birds in any season and her bird feeders jammed with visitors. The Cape has a good many berries and seeds, but as more and more building goes on, the natural food is scarcer and the birds depend on their humans.

By December there are only nine hours of daylight and fifteen of darkness. But the birds make the most of the short days. The animals who hibernate are perhaps luckier, for they survive on their stored fat whereas the birds must keep eating to maintain their body heat and survive.

I do not know how the rabbits manage but my yard is no longer carpeted with them. They vanish with the clover and fresh green rose leaves. But when it snows there are tracks of small beings I never see, all over the terrace. Sometimes I see a couple of grouse by Charlie Moore's pond and my friend Ed reports a red fox yapping. An occasional owl hoots from the woods above Duck Pond. But the world is generally full of stillness as winter moves along.

The road is no longer full of young quail when I drive to town. They are grown-ups now and will be leading their own offspring back and forth when days are warm again.

I always think of Thoreau on cold winter days, for I remember his describing walking the outer beach holding his open umbrella behind him to act as a kind of sail. He first came in 1849 and returned in 1855 and 1857. He took "public transportation" to Orleans and then walked to Provincetown.

It seems to me that aside from his fascination with the sea he was most impressed with how low the trees were. He keeps estimating the height of trees and shrubs. The incessant Cape winds may be responsible as well as the sandy soil (it can hardly be called soil). In some places the sand is mixed with a clayey deposit but below that is more sand. The rich loam is notable for its absence.

When my cousin Rob moved to Orleans he said he was going to plant a garden but knew it wouldn't be any use. Rob and I have a long heritage of true farmers and Rob was accustomed to raising vegetables in Massachusetts deep inland. Much to his surprise he found he could raise enough vegetables on the Cape to feed all of Orleans. The main problem is not the soil, for somehow seeds simply leap up. The problem is water, for it does not rain often enough and the light sandy soil is a sieve as far as holding moisture.

When we do get a three-day downpour, Rob says happily, "It's worth a hundred and fifty dollars, that rain."

The icy rains of winter tend to run off much of the time instead of filtering down to thirsty roots. But I notice the water table in the small ponds rises and this is a blessing, for during a summer drought, these ponds almost vanish.

Incidentally, Thoreau had no fear of pollution, for he was

always stopping to drink from a fresh-water pond! However, in 1849 I doubt whether any sewers emptied into them!

Thoreau felt the sand was the great enemy of the Cape, and as he sank to his ankles in it, he felt its power. He describes the early houses built on piles in the sand.

Since he was such a perceptive naturalist, he realized that cutting down the forests was a major reason for the vast barren areas with drifting sand. Nowadays sand fences are erected, pilings driven in on the back beach and cement blocks laid in. But, so far as I know, the experts have not been able to defeat the merciless tides of sand.

The dunes are magnificent, no matter how uncontrollable. Some hardy souls walk them in winter when the desolate sweep of waves thunders in on the back beach at Nauset. My dear friend Eileen is one of them. She is a gifted artist and she hunts for brine-blackened boards, driftwood, shells, tawny seaweed and cinnamon beach grass. From these treasures she creates works of art which give the essence of the Cape itself, with its mystery and magic.

Sometimes, from somewhere, tree roots are cast up, silvered by salt and wind and smoothed with the tides. From these Eileen makes lamps such as the one by their fireplace. I have several of the wall plaques and the three at Stillmeadow bring me the serenity of summer on the Cape as I look at them. The one at Still Cove is a composition of three clove-brown cattails, beach grasses, and a single blue butterfly. The base is a weathered rectangular inch-thick board, a gift from the sea.

When we first came to the Cape, the outer beaches were full of driftwood, but collectors have been busy down the years. It is harder to find every year. A few old-timers have ancient iron anchors and there is an arch over a gateway in Eastham made of a whalebone rib (I think it is his rib) but the beaches are no longer full of treasure trove.

A good many ships were wrecked on the bars in the very early days and the Cape Codders put the wreckage to good use, especially the ship timbers which were a help in building houses. Some beachcombers had the habit of lighting flares to misguide ships in trouble offshore so the ships would run aground. This worked better on dark nights and I am told the word *Mooncussers* derives from the fact the thieves cussed the moon.

The pheasants are scarcer than the quail. They feed early and again at dusk, with the dramatic males always ahead. They run with a peculiar skipping gait, and rise heavily as if getting airborne were a chore. The male is so bright he looks painted, and also the collar around his neck gives a kind of white tie and tails impression. There is one cock that runs along the road edge above Charlie Moore's pond, and I always stop the car and wait for him to get back into the brush, for both pheasants and quail tend to dart in front of cars when they are confused. But as I have said, the quail are the constant road-crossers, while the pheasant tends to keep on one side.

It is something to wonder at that the gulls, which are also heavy-bodied, can be airborne so easily and ride the air currents with scarcely any beating of their wings. When I have worked too long and feel tight with weariness, nothing rests me more than to look out at the gulls circling Mill Pond. I suddenly feel lightened and serene. The darting, swooping smaller birds sometimes give a sense of nervousness, but the gulls give a gift of quiet, even though their voices are harsh and desolate.

I like to watch the hawk who lives over toward Blue Rock but I do not find his power dive conducive to peace. There is something ominous about that wingspread so that I tend to identify with the small folk quivering in terror below.

Nauset Beach at night. (*John Schram*)

Last winter was a hard one for the birds, for the Cape had a long spell of freezing with some ice storms. My dear friends Ruth and Charlotte found birds frozen to death under their feeder more than once. I have never seen this in Connecticut even in the twenty below weather and wonder if it is because there is more cover in our swamp there, or whether the small bodies vanish in the deep drifts and some predators find them as soon as the melt begins. Their survival at all, ever, in a New England winter is a major miracle. Hal Borland tells me the circulation in the legs and feet is adjusted some way—they would freeze to the branches if they had our kind of warm-blooded extremities.

As the year turns toward Christmas, it is a time of homecoming. All over New England streets are decorated, store windows blaze with color, and Christmas trees go up in town centers. I think we push the season too much; it now begins right after Thanksgiving. It also is too commercial and too complicated so that most homemakers are exhausted by New Year's!

The shortest days come between the 17th and 26th, and short they are indeed. But the night sky is patterned with stars that seem brighter and the moon path on the water is white gold. The almanac predicted five degrees colder than normal and less snow in the Boston area. In the Connecticut area it forecast 50 percent less snow.

The children always long for a white Christmas, and snow does seem to belong to Christmas as roses belong to June. However, Christmas is an affair of the heart and a green Christmas is still the most blessed of holidays.

One of the nicest customs we have is that of Christmas wreaths on front doors and doorways garlanded with pine. And as we drive along the snowy streets, a good many houses have the Christmas trees by the front windows, so the colored lights shine out at dusk. The use of evergreens at this season symbolizes a renewal of faith and hope for a weary world, as do the traditional carols and the lighted candles.

Most of the Christmas trees nowadays are grown on tree farms, especially in the north. The ritual of the family going out to cut the tree from their own woods is seldom practiced. In the early days at Stillmeadow, Jill planted a big stand of Christmas trees but the only ones ever cut were cut by thieves and hauled away in the dead of night. If you plant a tree, I think, you are never going to want to cut it down, it is too beautiful reaching farther to the sky every year. It is better to buy the tree and comfort yourself by saying it has already been cut!

The problem of transportation to and from the Cape can be most difficult at the holidays. The railroad tracks once went all the way to Provincetown, but rail service is long gone. The only reminder is that some spots on the main route you drive down-Cape suddenly develop an accordion bounce which tends to toss backseat passengers into mid-air. The railroad crossed at these points, although I wonder just why . . .

It is still possible to buy some of the old railroad ties, and treasures they are, blackened solid lengths of timber. They have more uses than I can count, but I like best to see them as steps on a slope with perennials blossoming on either side and a piney glade at the top where the sea wind rests.

Now the bus replaces the train, but a good many people have difficulty finding Cape-bound busses from their own area. The planes fly in and out of Boston and also Hyannis, and small planes fly from Provincetown to Boston. In winter, when the Atlantic storms roar in, misadventures make up a good deal of the conversation over eggnogs.

"And there he was sitting at the wrong airport three hours. There just wasn't any way to reach him. He sat in the car."

"And Cindy finally did get in, but her luggage went on to Miami. So Bill had to make an extra trip to Boston and then, you won't believe it, but they gave him a record-player and it wasn't Cindy's at all but belonged to a friend so he had to go back to Boston to take the record-player—"

"They couldn't land at Hyannis and there we were—"

The Provincetown shuttle usually does get through, but of course Provincetown is the tip of the Cape and it may take an hour to get there unless you happen to be located nearby.

So the main transportation on the Cape is by private auto. Jimmy DeLory has a fine taxi service from Orleans with a smiling, gentle driver named Arthur who recently drove a sick child to Boston in the middle of the night, but families who come from inland generally pack children, dogs, kittens, luggage and the necessary adults into the family car and drive. Incidentally, many of the people I know who spend the winter months in Florida also drive back and forth. They report the trip takes about three days and is really not so bad.

Then I have one friend who takes the bus to New York when she has to go and survives a nine-hour trip with more patience than I would have.

Well, one way or another, relatives do manage to get to the Cape in time for Christmas Eve, carol singing, candlelight, the secret wrapping of packages, the roast pork or turkey, the hot buttered rum. And if Christmas Day is clear and sun-bright, the homecoming ones find time to just "take a look at the beach" or go over to check the fishing shack.

For the sea is deep in the bone-marrow and lungs are starved for the wild salt wind and, as the Cape Codders always say, "You need to get sand in your shoes."

The almanac calendar runs out and a new cycle begins, but nature sets her own sequence and we cannot regiment her. The sun inevitably swings north and days lengthen and at night the Wolf Moon of January rises across Mill Pond. The holiday parties are done and on Twelfth Night the greens are burned in the fireplace—and one distinctive characteristic of the Cape dwellers is that fire is always a hazard so the greens are burned in small pieces, and tissue paper and tinsel carefully disposed of.

The first of the year is generally bitter cold with an ice storm or a sifting of snow. The oil trucks make an extra trip and householders look nervously at the woodpiles. The juncos, chickadees, cardinals fill the yard with wings, and the small animals cross the steps to the beach. The catlike track of a fox appears by the road edge. And Amber is content to sit inside and look out!

Yesterday I went to Lilac Farm to visit with Helen Beals and her charming stepdaughter Kathy, and Kathy's gifted husband Rico. We sat in the living room and had just finished speaking of the British officers who sipped their rum there in 1812 when a terrible crash sent us spinning into the air. Conditioned as we are to our age, we felt sure a bomb had fallen on the ancient house.

"Someone has crashed," said Rico, rushing to the front hall.

I began to think one of the giant elms must have fallen on the roof. But Rico called, "Don't worry. It is just that the ceiling has collapsed."

We tiptoed into the hall and saw the staircase deep with plaster and the upper hall knee-high with debris.

Apparently some of the heavy rains had found a convenient leak in the roof, and water from the attic was responsible. While Helen called a builder friend, we found enough common sense to be thankful nobody was upstairs at the time. I remembered once in the 1690 house inland one small chunk of plaster fell in an upstairs bedroom, but I had never been in a house when the whole ceiling fell and can report it did indeed sound like a bomb. The man who patched the piece at Stillmeadow was enchanted by the ancient plaster held together with horsehair, and by the hand-cut lathe underneath, and I was bemused by the idea of how enough horsehair was collected in that period for all the early houses in the valley.

I thought of the old saying that a man's house is his castle, but I added, only with the help of plumbers, electricians, painters and carpenters. Every house is a composite of the skilled labor which has made it that castle.

I have been fortunate enough to watch the career of a young builder in Orleans. Bobby was a thin, shy, ten-year-old when he first came into my life. I think he was on his way to the beach and stopped to say hello because I was out in the yard with Holly. Later, when he was in high school, we had some struggles with his English course. My efforts to infuse his spirit with a passion for poetry were not exactly a success.

We could watch a sunset blazing in the sky and I would choose a special poem to fit.

"Well, why doesn't he just say the sun was setting?" Bobby would ask sensibly.

On the other hand, he was amazed at my profound ignorance (that is the only way to describe it) of mathematics and wasted a good many pads of paper trying to show me how easy and sensible math was!

We rested from these bouts with folk records and pizzas.

And all the time this quiet gray-eyed boy was setting his course. He crossed the bridge for a brief time to go to Tech but he could not breathe inland air. Summers he worked at the lobster shop and this may have been a mistake, for he has been cleaning and filleting all the fish for family and friends ever since. His father Jim is a champion fisherman and enjoyed leaving the catch for Bobby.

When he went to work for a carpenter, he suddenly grew

taller. His shoulders broadened and some of his shyness vanished. Every detail of building was exciting. On his days off he never had time to water-ski because he was building shelves for my kitchen cupboard, doing some remodeling in his family's house, helping neighbors fix leaky roofs.

And then one day he said casually, "I am going to be a builder."

We watched his first house go up, designed and built by him, and to me outdoing Camelot. Last summer, his ninety-thousand-dollar one was gorgeous but that first one can never be equaled.

Along the way he courted and won the charming, intelligent daughter of very dear friends and at the moment has just finished the home for his wife and baby son, a dream house in the piney woods.

As I think about this particular success story, I feel it is as much a part of what America is all about as the aimless, drug-dazed, long-haired youngsters are. This is still a land of opportunity, I am sentimental enough to believe. If the lost boys and girls could have a dream and a goal, and any kind of a constructive aim, their story would have a different ending. So far as it looks, they have no interest in building, only in tearing down.

In my own life, I have been blessed by close and enduring friendships and abiding affection of five teenage boys—all from the age of ten on to manhood. David, Jill's son, grew up at Stillmeadow. Tommy and Erwin have been daily members of the household. Richard Lovely was a Cape neighbor and Bobby lived around the corner of Mill Pond Road. Perhaps in an earlier age, they would have been just intelligent, delightful boys but today they seem incredible examples!

I have a strange reaction to this, for as I think how I cherish them, I feel an overwhelming compassion for the teenagers I see sitting on the benches by the old cemetery in the center of Orleans. They have nowhere to go, nothing to do but steal enough for another round of grass. Their bare feet encrusted with dirt, their hair stiff with sweat, their psychedelic pants ripped, sweatshirts stained, they are, I admit, a revolting sight. But underneath the exterior, somewhere, deep inside is just another youngster desperately in need of something never given.

The antidote for my grief is to listen to Bobby as he describes making paneling by hand for the next house, using seventy-five kegs of nails for roofing, and finding mellowed old bricks for a fireplace!

"New bricks just don't have the same look," he says.

I no longer bother because I never could teach him poetry, for he finds his own in dentil moldings, hand-pegged floors and graceful doorways. As well as what he calls sexy bathrooms, which means gay colors and elegant cabinets!

So far, none of the experts I have listened to have cleared up my confusion about the troubled youth of today. The war in Vietnam is an easy answer and the fact that our other wars were for a defendable reason (if war ever can be) and this cannot be rationalized the same way, is not the whole story. One theory is that parents are complete failures, but I wonder whether parents haven't always just fumbled along as best they could. Democracy cannot be the main culprit, if Cuba, Russia and China are examples of ideal governments.

Overpopulation probably has something to do with the situation, for there are not enough jobs and the cities are jammed with slums and ghettos. Education has not been as good as it should be—but it never was, as far as I know. At least, in this country children are supposed to go to school and can read anything they want in the libraries without being put in jail as subversives.

But in this wide land there are still uncrowded sections with playgrounds, athletic fields for Junior Leaguers, churches that are attended, job opportunities. The Cape has many advantages aside from her natural beauty, but is not the only area where life can be worthwhile.

The last census (1970) set the Cape population at something around eighty-eight thousand with a summer influx of around one or two hundred thousand. So far, there are more jobs on the Cape than men and women to fill them. The theme song is always HELP WANTED. And there are no real slum areas. New schools are always going up, including a much-needed technical school. Yet even here, the police raids net houses full of drug addicts, and store windows are smashed from time to time.

So the tide of trouble rises in this serene narrow land and there is no escape from it. It will ebb, I have faith to believe, for our country has a way of surviving!

Amber does not go out in winter, since she is allergic to cold. The one time she slipped out of an open door she landed on a film of ice and her efforts to keep all four paws in the air while getting back inside were spectacular. She is happy to sit on the windowsill swiveling her head around following the fall of snowflakes or making that clicking sound at the cardinals and chickadees.

But she is not an idle cat. The typical pictures of cats dozing by the fire do not fit her. Instead, the minute I settle down at the typewriter for a good serious session, she decides to leap to the top bookshelf, right next to the ceiling, and then swing from the drapery valance. Or she soars into the air and lands in the midst of my precious Limoges china. This is supposed to be off limits, so she folds herself up in about three inches of space and turns a bland gaze at me.

"See me! Didn't even knock off a teacup," she says quite plainly.

She doesn't exactly lack for exercise, and neither do I as I scoop her from the refrigerator top (there is room to fall down behind) or retrieve her from the washing machine before the water is turned on!

Then around holiday time when gifts of flowers and plants arrive, I keep a wary eye to be sure she doesn't feel like eating a leaf or two or picking the rose petals off. I am careful of big brown paper bags since the time I picked one up and started for the dump with it. It seemed heavy for torn envelopes and used paper towels. When I realized five pounds of cat was in it, I had to sit down to recover.

One noncat friend remarked that I must be nervous chasing after Amber. But I assured her there was nothing so restful as a cat, and this is true. At those times when the world seems to be falling in shreds, I will see my gentle angel fast asleep in a block of sunshine on the softest pillow in the house. Paws folded under, tail packaging the recumbent form and small wedge-shaped face tucked under one wrist, she is serenity distilled. I feel the tensions ebb in my bones. That desperate feeling we all get that it is impossible to catch up vanishes. The long list of undone chores seems nonessential. The unfinished chapter hanging from the typewriter can wait until tomorrow.

What do I do? I ease myself gently down on the sofa and just touch the soft-breathing form, feeling the rise and fall of that breathing and letting my fingers rest on the incredibly delicate fur. Sometimes she opens one eye and gives me one of those profound looks, then sighs.

And somehow her quiet brings everything in the world into focus.

When I think about it, I feel sure the ability to relax completely is a gift mankind needs, and those of us who are intimate with animals are fortunate enough to share it. I watch a miniature dachshund puppy explode all over the Lovelys' kitchen, pouncing, lunging, spinning. Then suddenly he collapses in his box, goes limp as a fallen leaf and is instantly asleep. The world is still strange to him, at twelve weeks, full of good and bad experiences, and learning to cope with it is an immense job. But when he rests, he rests with his whole tiny self; his only contact with existence is to keep breathing!

I have seen an entire litter of eight-week-old cocker puppies in a maelstrom of activity all at once, in unison, tumble into a heap and lie so motionless I worried whether they would ever wake up at all. And Holly used to levitate up the steep bank from beach to house after racing on the sand and swimming and chasing rabbits and fall into deep slumber as soon as she got to her side of the sofa. Holly, however, dreamed. Her mahogany tail would beat, her soft lips quiver, paws twitch. If Amber dreams, she does not show it.

For the experts who are so feverishly trying to analyze sleep by wiring electrodes and such to people, I would suggest an easy definition of sleep. Sleep is an Abyssinian kitten on a pillow in the sunshine!

Memory is a strange affair, for often it is not voluntary. Trying to remember a name or a place or a forgotten line of a favorite sonnet or the ingredients of a recipe or how to get to a difficult place like the Johnsons' in Wellfleet—these are voluntary engagements with memory.

But there are those other risings from deep down that seem to come by themselves. I cannot explain why on a cold winter day as I drove down Tonset past the meadow on the left, I looked at the icy expanse and suddenly saw the purple vetch in bloom in early July, covering the area with color. I seemed to smell honeysuckle and feel the air feather-soft.

Another day, at sunset, Millie and Ed and I came down Bridge Road from Eastham past the salt marsh, rusty brown and lifeless, and I recaptured it suddenly in summer when the marsh grass glows a brilliant emerald laced with silver ribbons of the tidal streams.

I had never consciously told myself to remember this but it was tucked away in the mysterious depths of memory. And something evoked it without conscious effort. It reminded me never to take any bit of beauty as a matter of course, but to absorb it and let it emerge whenever it wills.

With regard to remembering consciously, I note that some people seem to hoard unpleasant memories and live with them. They can talk endlessly about unfortunate happenings or troubles fate has visited upon them, and I must say get a great deal of ego-satisfaction from them. Recently I spent some time with a friend I had not seen for a number of years. As I sank slowly under the weight of every misfortune she had been through, I began to wonder whether one or two happy things might have been hers. Surely someone must have done a kind thing or lent a helping hand, but in the end my conclusion was that she would never see her roses, only the Japanese beetles.

The day I enjoyed the blossoming vetch in January, I took the long road home down Brick Hill Road in search of another memory. Last June my cousin Rob and I drove that way and Rob suddenly stopped the car.

"Just look at that!" he said.

Both of us had been down that road countless times, but now we saw for the first time the whole road edge jeweled with rosy pink. Rob bounced out (he is a very bouncy man) and bent over.

"The leaves look like locust—or maybe sweet pea," he said. "Do you know what this is?"

"You are the botanist," I reminded him.

He gently pulled one handful of the blossoms and brought them over.

A marsh creek in winter. (*John Schram*)

"They have to be sweet peas, wild sweet peas," I said. "Those are definitely pea blossoms. I think they may be beach peas."

"Maybe I better dig up a clump for us before the town mows this strip," Rob said.

Of course he never did, but we had examined that one blossoming spray carefully. Now, in winter, I slowed down around that curve and remembered that summer day, but I was consciously dredging up the memory. It was not at all like seeing the vetch and the marsh grass. The road edge was deep with fallen leaves and dead grass and the air had the knife-sharpness and smelled of snow.

My final conclusion, as I turned down Mill Pond Road, was that it takes a lifetime to wonder about our own inner selves, our thoughts and feelings and perceptions, and I cannot imagine anyone ever being bored!

At night, I see only an occasional light on the shore of Robert's Cove, which leads to the big water. Most of the houses are closed and the owners scattered all over inland. The empty houses are visible at midday but just why they look so obviously empty, I do not know. But there is a different kind of stillness about a closed house from one whose owners are off all day to the beach. And when you drive around town, there is a special glow about those whose people have not left them.

Houses have personalities, I think, and most of them are social-minded. Occasionally one enters a house that has no welcome. The air inside seems rigid. The furniture is lifeless. The windows stare blankly at the intruder. But this is rare, for most houses want to be lived in and cherished. A winter-closed house gives the effect of mournfulness.

When I have to leave Still Cove, Millie and Ed give it companionship, walking over from Champlain Road and playing a few records while they look out at Mill Pond. And Stillmeadow, in summer, bubbles with excitement as children and friends and various pets take over.

In Orleans, as on most of the Cape, there are watch services—men who check closed houses regularly. This is a relatively new feature, since vandalism arrived on the Cape. Stories of breaking-and-entering make conversation as soon as summer ends. One woman came back to find someone had been living in her house.

"I'll never get over it!" she said. "They didn't steal anything except some canned food, but they left lipstick on my best sheets—lipstick all over them!"

One friend and her husband got in late one night after a long journey and had what seems to me the worst welcome of all. A raccoon had come down the chimney and clawed everything to bits, spreading chimney soot on walls and floors and all over the freshly painted bathroom.

"I said we had better give up the house," said my friend, "and start over somewhere else."

I wasn't very popular when I said how dreadful it was for the trapped coon!

The winter the Hong Kong flu hit Cape Cod, the inhabitants were doubly stricken. Not only was the epidemic a fierce one but the very idea that the Cape should have it *at all* was hard to take. Of course it was imported from across the bridge, everyone said. There is a strong feeling that anything undesirable on the Cape has been BROUGHT IN.

The various kinds of weeds came with the Pilgrims from England, in their stores and luggage. Ticks (the Cape's worst problem) were imported by way of Belgian hares. And most viruses come from city areas by way of tourists. But even this sea-girt Paradise cannot be isolated from the rest of the country, and it is also true that the Cape could not be self-support-

ing if it were sealed off. The trucks that roll down the Mid-
Cape highway bring everything from food products to
television sets. As of now, the Cape must even import some of
its lobsters from Boston.

And the summer visitors keep the economy stabilized.

Like most areas in the United States, the problem of medical service is acute, and during the Hong Kong flu, patients
simply stayed in bed at home and swallowed the pills delivered from the drugstores after telephone conversations with
the doctors. The doctors were flat out.

The situation is curious here on the narrow land, for the
few doctors are so overburdened that their patients worry
constantly about THEM. As far as possible, we try to save our
doctors and simply wait to "throw it off" instead of asking
for a house call. Fortunately, during the past few years, several new dentists have come to town and it is now possible to
get a tooth filled without waiting two weeks. And, as I write,
everyone is celebrating the arrival of a new pediatrician to
share the load of the other one.

But the medical problem is universal in this country and
the days are gone when the family doctor could drop in and
stay half an hour or more, and by his very presence make the
patient feel better. A good many articles of late have been
written about it and a documentary about a community in
the middle west with no doctor who could be found, but the
main reason is seldom spoken of. Having helped educate Jill's
son as a doctor, I find the problem simple. It costs too much
and takes too long. Many young men who would wish to
serve as doctors cannot afford the ballooning expense nor the
time interning when, if they marry, the wives must support
them and children have to be deferred.

So we muddle along and sympathize with patients who
cannot have a vitally necessary operation for several weeks
because the surgeon has no free operating time. The hospitals

keep on building wings, such as the one at Hyannis, but they are battling against odds.

Recently in Boston an experiment began, using closed-circuit television for patients and doctors. The patient only sees a nurse actually, as the interview is broadcast. This is supposed to save time and be more efficient and it may well be that before long impersonal machinery will diagnose and treat the ill.

I doubt whether it will work. Any patient like me would give up when the first light flashed on the screen. My idea is that one begins to feel better after a short visit with the pretty and sympathetic office nurse. It is pleasant to chat while waiting for the doctor, exchanging family news.

The doctor begins by asking how the book is going and how many pages are left to do. A brief discussion of books and some comments on the political situation follow. All the time he is observing, estimating, and all the time I feel better and better. By the time the check-up is over, I sally forth without an ache or pain.

Of course this is not as fast as a computerized appointment, it takes time, but healing is a personal affair and most of us would never feel a machine could replace a man.

"Well, I have an appointment for a check-up," says a neighbor in June. "I'm so lucky—he can fit me in by the end of August."

My own Cape doctor works day and night and has a vacation when he gets sick himself. The nearest hospital is the one in Hyannis and going back and forth consumes a great deal of time. This hospital serves an area where three might manage satisfactorily. But money comes into the situation again, for even a hospital wing seems to cost a million dollars.

Perhaps it is unfortunate that we are a nation of health-conscious people and consider doctors as minor gods. In an earlier generation, everything could be cured by sending off a few dollars for medicines that cured everything from heart trouble to tuberculosis and you diagnosed your ailment and sent the order. Studying an ancient mail-order catalogue, I noticed all of the medicines that were liquid, as most were, had up to 26 percent alcohol, which probably made the consumers feel better no matter what!

There was a period in our early days in Connecticut when the community had no doctor, but we had a fine veterinarian in New Haven and Jill always said we could consult him if we got sick!

In any case, I imagine most doctors feel disheartened as they work so desperately to battle illness and realize at the same time that 42,900 young healthy men have been killed in another kind of battle.

One bright note in the picture on-Cape is the excellence of the Rescue Squad as well as the Coast Guard. In case of accidents on land or sea, the speed with which help comes is miraculous.

"If I had a heart attack," says one friend, "I'd hope to have it at the market, for the Rescue Squad would be there in ten minutes!"

The police are always ready too with first aid, and the town nurse is always on the job and is a rock and refuge for a good many people.

There are rumors that two or three new doctors may move into the area and this would be a major blessing. Meanwhile it is a good idea to avoid head-on collisions and falling off ladders or rowing a leaky boat out in a Nor'easter. In short, be careful.

Most of the accidents on the water are due to sheer carelessness. For instance, a small outboard boat will be loaded with twice as many passengers as it should hold. Life jackets are forgotten as the craft heads out to sea. The motor stalls, one oar is lost, and the boat is soon swamped. Then, instead of hanging to the boat, the people start to swim toward shore, making rescue almost impossible.

The rule for water-skiing is that one person must sit facing the skier, at the back of the boat. The helmsman gets directions from a man sitting at the bow. Too often nobody keeps watch at the rear and if the skier gets in trouble, he is dragged under water as the boat lunges ahead.

What is really surprising is that there are so few casualties!

There is a woodchuck living down the bank toward Mill Pond. I can see the opening to his burrow, marked by a sloping patch of raw dirt. I never see him, but Amber assures me he is still there, for she sits and stares fixedly at the burrow for twenty minutes at a time. Someday I wish his funny face would poke out of the hole and we could watch him ambling off. But up to date the only chuck I have seen was over by Charlie Moore's pond and I think that is too far away for him to be my friend.

We know so little about the small mammals not far from our doorsteps. Why do some hibernate and some not? What mysterious laws of nature make some able to live on stored fat and some struggle in ice and snow to scrounge a thin living? And why do the alewives battle their way up herring run to spawn? Some think the fresh water is better for the eggs, but why is it? Some think the pools when they survive to reach them have a better temperature or provide more shelter. Or they are safer from the predatory gulls and other enemies. If this be their motive, they couldn't be more mistaken, for barrels of them are scooped up as they flash in beauty in the shallow water.

I think one fisherman summed it up, "It is God's plan."

We dwell surrounded by mystery. Those fortunate enough to live outside the cities do have more time to observe the habits of nature and perhaps keep a wider outlook. Cape people all seem to be willing to take time out from anything to watch and think. And what makes news might not seem world-shaking, but when a friend sees some fox kits, we can discuss it for a long time!

And when I go out with Amber in summer and every songbird in the area perches on treetips around us and utters warning curses so she sits paralyzed. This is neighborhood news for some time!

The Cape Codder's feeling for nature is bone-deep and is especially endearing. Living with the sea around them has much to do with it, I think. It is the only place I have lived where the man who comes to balance the pump will stand motionless for some time, leaning on the split-rail fence and looking at the water.

"Just look at that view," he says.

The milkman reports the Canada geese are here. The young man who mows what isn't really a lawn stops to admire the diving ducks and the blossoming lilacs. There is a closeness to sky and sea which makes me pray the narrow land will never be destroyed by bulldozers or the clear waters filled with sewage or the life-giving marshes all filled in.

One reason there is always time to absorb the beauty is that the tempo of life on the Cape is, let us say frankly, slow. Nobody runs when they can walk. What doesn't get done one day may get done the next or the next. Nervous breakdowns from living under pressure are not usual. Newcomers often get fretful as they wait endlessly for plumbers, electricians or carpenters, but once they fall into the pattern, they live longer. Faces are etched by sea wind, browned by sun, but tension lines tend to disappear.

The very immensity of the sea brings a sense of tranquillity, and sunset at Rock Harbor brings a kind of eternity to the spirit. Workmen sit in their trucks quietly watching the sun turn the water to fire, and beachcombers stand and stare, dazzled by the light.

Out of season the Cape is quiet, too, without the ear-splitting noise of the city or suburbia. The noon whistle downtown does make me jump but it does not last very long. At night Main Street is silent with only a few lights on and the occasional sound of a motor at the gas station. Almost everything closes at nine o'clock, when people ought to be at home anyway unless they go to the movie.

It never pays to be too sure about people. We all, I think, do tend to peg them and be assured that our ideas are right. Today I went to the flower shop and found a new African violet, midnight purple, imported from Germany—Rhapsodie. With a note that propagating it is strictly *verboten*.

The next thing I realized was that Mr. Bill, the impersonal florist, was leaning his long elegance against the counter, his handsome face framed in a sheath of rosy gladioli.

"You've got plenty of African violet food, Gladys," he remarked. "You don't need the special kind they recommend. They're all the same anyway."

Then we had an intimate discussion of African violets, their personality and habits!

So, after all, we were friends at long last, on a first-name basis! I hummed all the way home, and when I settled the violet plant in, it looked even lovelier. I somehow felt triumphant. For on the narrow land, people do not use first names unless they mean it.

I think we all have an identity with our first name, an odd basic emotion which may have come down from the dawn of civilization. We *are* our names, in a way. It was a strange period when wives in America addressed their husbands as Mister, no doubt a form of respect and an admission husbands were not to be trifled with.

Then I have been in big-city communities where nobody seemed to have a last name at all. "This is Gladys," was my introduction. "I know you'll enjoy Tom."

I never liked this, any more than I like being addressed as Mrs. Taber all the time. For it didn't imply anything by way of acquaintance. The first time I went to a big cocktail party (fresh from the middle west) and people I never had laid eyes on, and probably wouldn't again, called me Gladys, I felt a strong distaste. They didn't know me from Adam, as my mother would say.

But what a pleasure after five or six years to reach first-name status with my friend Bill!

It is not really possible to pigeonhole people in various parts of the United States. For one thing, we are a peripatetic nation. The Pilgrims have been described endlessly as rigid, narrow, determined men and women, humorless and never fun-loving. There was only one right way, and that was theirs. But nobody ever questions their courage and their will to survive. And underneath the stern exterior they loved and suffered and hoped and dreamed as mankind has always done.

The Cape Codders of today have a fine rich vein of humor and are certainly more tolerant, but sometimes I find echoes of the early folk when some controversial issue comes up in Town Meetings. They do not exactly reason together but they do shout a lot. And every voter knows his viewpoint is the only right one. Afterward things go on as before when the anger simmers down.

Among my personal friends, I notice one area of agreement, which is that money is not for spending but for saving. Newcomers who happen to be overly blessed with the world's goods are under suspicion until they live this down.

"What do you expect from anyone with all that money?" I hear often. And then, "The M's are just as nice as anybody in spite of all that income. Real good people."

I have lived in many parts of the United States where having money was the status symbol and also in some where being descended from old families was the only important thing. But on Cape Cod, so far as I can figure out, a man's basic quality is what matters. Although it is a help if one can be a descendant of the Nickersons or Eldredges or Snows. I sometimes find myself explaining timidly about my own ancestors, their connection with Harvard and witches and so on, although what this has to do with my own worth I cannot decide!

I do remember my grandmother's feeling that it was almost a sin that I was not born in Massachusetts.

The snow began in the flat silence of predawn. It fell idly with disarming slowness. By the time I got up, a faint haze of white lay on the junipers and Mill Pond edges were lacy.

"Well, this won't amount to anything," said my neighbor Ed. "It will be gone by noon. But I'll bring your mail."

By noon it was still snowing and I noticed something unlike most inland snows, for the flakes seemed to fall horizontally as if they did not come down from the sky but were born somewhere over the dunes. The house grew cold suddenly and Amber sat by the bathroom heat grill behind the bathroom door. I turned up the furnace and put on a sweater and heated hearty vegetable beef soup for lunch.

Ed's boots made tracks in the yard and his storm jacket glittered with stars. There was no wind and the tide moved in soundlessly. The gulls vanished, the Canada geese drifted to the small duck pond. The diving ducks sought shelter. By afternoon a faint pink light seemed to come from the snow itself. Was it because of the expanse of sea that was never lightless or the open vast of sky? I had never seen anything like it. Mill Pond itself was slate-colored and empty as grief.

All that night the snow came down, and all the next day. I

was snowed in! At Stillmeadow I expect this in February and keep the house stocked with supplies in a regular routine, but who expected this on Cape Cod (the Florida of New England)? It seemed unreal. Amber curled up on the warmest end of the sofa and insulated herself with a firmly wrapped tail. I warmed her milk and turned the furnace up again. By now it quivered in protest.

The next morning, the snow finally ceased. When I looked out of the big picture windows I saw the intricate patterns of nameless wild folk on the rippled snow. It was as if the snow tried to imitate the sea and one expected the ripples to move toward an unseen shore. The design of the tracks was unlike any inland, for they did not seem to be going anywhere, simply crossing and recrossing. Amber studied them with interest, but neither of us knew who had been there. Her nose is needle-sharp and I opened the door far enough so she could get any scent there might be.

I was housebound four days. From the windows I looked out at the frosted junipers, masses of them, and the jack pines dipped in silver. It was like a series of magnified Christmas cards, which always seem so artificial.

That afternoon Millie came over and I felt like someone on a desert island first sighting a sail. We had coffee and warm conversation, after which she struggled down the outside cellar steps (there are no inside ones unfortunately) and brought up the snow shovel Margaret Stanger gave me last fall as a going-away present. She was still scraping away when Ed, her husband, turned up and also negotiated the cellar and found the turf edger and chopped at the ice by the front stoop. When they were all through, Ed advised me not to go outside until it melted a little.

When I did get out, a day later, the town glittered in the sharp sun. The lovely ancient houses seemed asleep, with nothing moving except the shadows across the still-white yards. I began to sing my usual tuneless song, "Oh beautiful Cape Cod—oh beautiful Cape Cod!" I wished I could share the beauty of light falling on the clapboards, for the etching of shadow under each one is wonderful to see. The dreamlike quality has a special charm. It rests the spirit and the quiet is like music.

By the time I got home, Mill Pond was awake. Nine Canada geese stood on their heads in the water, feeding to make up for lost time. Their undersides are white and shone in the new sun. The blue heron fished at the edge of the small pond.

A deceptive warmth gentled my bones. Winter was over at last. That snow must be a permanent farewell! And, as is usual on the Cape, two days were sweet with the promise of spring. March began on Sunday and from the cars parked by the churches, women blossomed forth in pinks and blues and golds. Open doors of the sanctuaries welcomed them to the security of faith.

But midweek the sky darkened over the ocean and cold air knifed in. I drove over to Rock Harbor and saw something I do not see inland. It was snowing and at the same time the sun shone through the clouds so there were pools of light on the silvery sand. The car radio gave the report for Plymouth, Cape Cod and the offshore islands. "Snow showers and small-craft warning. Lows in the twenties at night."

Patches of forget-me-not-blue sky appeared as the clouds drifted toward tomorrow. But the old lightship was curtained with snowflakes. It was low tide and the wet sand took the snowfall and it vanished, but the honey-pale fringes of beach sand were frosted.

There was a timeless quality invading my heart. So this must have looked when the ice age was over. Even now the few giant boulders reaching from the water had a look of eternity. I reflected they are the autographs from countless ages past. How small today and tomorrow seem, measured against them.

What is man, that thou art mindful of him?

I had been full of problems. The furnace was acting up again. The storm windows rattled. The kitchen sink had a dripping faucet. My favorite turquoise pin was missing. Too many bills came in the mail. And some checks had not come in. The mechanics of living seemed just too much to cope with.

But now they seemed inconsequential. I had a Thoreau-like feeling of being free of civilization (if we can call it that in this age). What did they matter measured against sky and sea and sun and snow?

What is Cape Cod?

It is an amethyst glow at the horizon over Mill Pond, announcing dawn.

It is the Full Flower Moon in May walking in gold on quiet water.

It is intrepid fishermen setting out in small boats in wind and waves.

It is the same boats rocking gently at anchor in the opal sunset harbor.

Shadblow and beach plum in drifts of snow followed by wild wide-petaled roses on every slope, these are Cape Cod.

Honey locusts and honeysuckle weighing the air with sweetness and sea lavender signing the beaches with delicate purple, these are Cape Cod.

Mockingbirds singing, song sparrows caroling from four in the morning to nine at night, goldfinches flashing yellow against the dark green pines, mourning doves grieving endlessly on every telephone wire, these are Cape Cod.

It is measuring a strawberry from Falmouth and finding it is four-and-a-half inches around it. And taking three bites to eat it, staining one's fingers with the dark rosy juice.

Tying up for the night. (*John Schram*)

It is neighbors. It is Pret Barker dripping on the doorsill with a
bucket of steamers, Jim Gibson sharing fresh-caught bass and
flounder, Ruth Walker and Charlotte Webber stopping by
with their gourmet liver aspic paté.

It is Ed Connors blowing in during a hurricane just to be sure
everything is all right.

It is stopping at the sight of Mr. Chapin flat on the ground and
finding out he is simply lying down to let his catbirds eat rai-
sins more comfortably out of his hand.

It is Shirley and Ginny calling to say there is something rather
special for supper and come on over.

It is the dark-eyed girl at the drive-in window at the bank who
always handed out a dog biscuit for one Irish setter along with
the cashed checks.

And it is Jimmy DeLory.

It is a straggling Memorial Day Parade in driving rain with the
marchers sloshing valiantly along toward the monument.

It is the patrol car at midnight cruising down to the Town Landing on Mill Pond.

It is all the memories of the girls, Jimmy, Bernice, Jeannine, who
save a comfortable table and ask about the kitten and how the
book is going, and Lois who stops to talk about where she got
her last exquisite costume, and Lib Trask at the bookstore with
her soft voice and lovely face.

It is Dick Dennison at the dump advising he will take care of the
trash—sit tight—no worry.

It is sitting in the sun in Barbara Lovely's yellow-and-delphinium
kitchen and holding a miniature dachshund puppy no bigger
than a teacup while Robin sits on a counter tuning her guitar
and Peter lugs four gallons of white paint down cellar and
Slim, the lord of the manor, has doffed his hospital garb and
donned paint-stained pants and a sweatshirt and vanishes to the
garden.

It is the flurry of arrival of Helen and Vicky filling the house
with gaiety and news of the world across the bridge.

It is two grandchildren, ten and eight, toiling up the steps from
the beach with arms full of sea treasures, damp and smelling of
dead fish and seaweed.

It is a hurricane warning with instructions as to evacuation. Bulletins continuous.

It is lobster rolls for a picnic with Philbrick's fried onion rings.

It is trying hopelessly to park so as to get into the Dennis Playhouse and squeezing into a seat in the remodeled barn to watch Shirley Booth bring her luminous quality to a play.

And it is a four-and-a-half-foot water snake coiling his way across the terrace while suddenly no bird sings.

All of these, and much more, are Cape Cod.

The golden days of summer end. There is sadness in the air as friends and relatives overload their cars and begin the long drive to Wisconsin and New Jersey and Washington. Goodbye—goodbye.

It is life drawing in during the long mellow days of autumn and schedules returning to the momentum of quiet communities with open roads and plenty of parking space.

It is meeting friends at Kristina's for permanents to repair the summer damage and to bask in Kristina's presence while her soft Irish voice eases the fatigue of the season.

It is David Constant, the landscape man, finally having time enough to plant bulbs and make one more attempt to save the wild cranberry slope by the east side of the house. Thinned to a pencil width from putting in lawns for new houses all season, he bends his dark head over the tangle of witch grass, and he works feverishly with the intensity of the young with a purpose. But even he stops to look out at Mill Pond and watch a little boat being loaded on a trailer. His narrow profile catches the late afternoon light. The boat rides awkwardly up the road and the curve swallows her up. David sighs and wrenches at a last patch of weeds. We both are aware that he will never finish the garden patch before winter, but we can pretend.

Dick Smith also is Cape Cod as he crawls around in the attic locating the leak. Before the Nor'easters the roof must be battened down. Frantic householders have been breathing down his neck for months, but now he can sit and have a cold drink and talk about his philosophy of life before he goes home to one of those fabulous spaghetti suppers his wife has ready.

Cape Cod is hard-working men with no idea of amassing large
sums of money, and Cape Cod is above all the wives. They answer the telephone at all hours, take emergency messages, lo-
cate the men if it is really imperative. They discuss symptoms
with great understanding, such as which button better be
pushed to stop the dishwasher flooding or cut off the oil
burner or keep the pump from pumping the well dry. They remind me of nurses on the front line and it is as rare for them
not to answer the phone. They must shop and take the children various places but somehow they answer the phone and
know where Larry Baker is and when he will be back and say
he will call. It was a minor crisis when Larry Leonard, the
wonderful electrician, changed his office and the wrong number was printed in the paper. For a long time Larry ran correc-
tions in the *Cape Codder* and *Oracle*. During the difficult time,
I was fortunate enough to meet him at the post office and that
solved my problems.

What is Cape Cod? It is a narrow stretch of land jutting into the
fathomless sea and so far man has not been able to devastate it
so it is as beautiful as young love's fragile dreaming.
But it is, in actuality, the people who sweep the pine pollen from
their doorsteps in season, carry a pot of home-baked beans to a
neighbor, knock themselves out finding a home for lost kittens,
feed crippled seagulls, fight fiercely at Town Meetings.
Cape Cod has back-biting, meanness, egotism, prejudice, hatred.
Human failings are not automatically purged by residence this
side of the bridge. Vandalism, thievery, arson are here. Jealousy
and selfishness exact their price.
But the stream of life flows clear, with the dregs seldom surfac-
ing. The sea herself is an eternal reminder of how small man is
and how good a wide horizon.
Cape Cod is whatever one seeks.

Epilogue

All of us experience life in whatever place circumstance or fate, if you will, has established us. Much of what we become grows from emotions and attitudes acquired from our home-place (I am sorry to repeat *place* but it is basic). We have advanced far enough in understanding to realize that slums and ghettos and our ghastly Indian reservations foster the growth of hatred and desperation. We don't do much about it, but at least we don't believe a poverty-stricken, rat-infested environment stimulates boys and girls to become dynamic, constructive leaders.

The fortunate look back to happy childhoods, urban, suburban or rural. They relate to a dream, and usually try to recapture the magic by settling in a location "just like where I grew up." This can be anywhere from the old Greenwich Village in New York City to a wheat farm in Minnesota, from Brooklyn Heights to Winnebago, Wisconsin.

Writers, even, who produce books which capitalize on the horrors of their home town have, I think, a secret love for it. They remind me of parents who beat their children for their own good.

My own childhood had no roots until I was in eighth grade. My memories are of packing and unpacking, riding endlessly in trains (grit and smoky smell and scratchy seats), being dumped briefly in a Mexican school, then in an Illinois one, then missing school. Father was a mining engineer and geologist and from California to Chihuahua we went. I still tell the grandchildren that when I was asked where I lived, I said, "On the train."

By the time Father settled down to being the head of the geology department at Lawrence, I had four years in one school and we had a house he built on the riverbank to live in. I had an Irish setter and a bicycle and my starved sterile roots went down deep in the rich Wisconsin soil.

We spent summers at Grandfather's farm in West Springfield, Massachusetts, where the relatives worked diligently to correct my dreadful accent. My tongue was indeed polyglot, although by then I had forgotten the Mexican Spanish.

After I married, I spent seven years in Virginia with the blue-black mountains rising at the edge of town and the mockingbirds singing and roses, roses, roses. Later, circumstance dropped me in a New York City apartment in a shabby old building near Columbia. From there to a 1690 farmhouse on thirty-eight acres of wooded land in rural Connecticut was the ultimate goal. There my cherished friend, Jill, and I settled down to raise our children after we lost our husbands. The record of country life in an ancient farmhouse with three children, a bevy of cockers, cats and at one time thirteen hens has been set down in the Stillmeadow books.

Then one day we came to see Cape Cod, on the theory that we hadn't had a vacation since we could remember and the children were away at college and a friend would stay with the cockers and cats and Irish. What a small hinge, I afterward thought, makes a door to open!

The first weekend cottage we built was just that and the winterized house followed inevitably, since we had plenty of land. Someday, we promised ourselves, we could retire to the one-floor easy-care (what a mistake!) house and turn the farm over to the children and grandchildren. Plans are a good thing to have on hand but these ended with Jill's untimely death. I found myself with two houses and learned that when one furnace gives out, the other inevitably collapses the same week!

I spend part of the year in each place and find the main problem is that half of the book I am working on is always at the wrong end. From the Cape, I call the farm and ask my son-in-law, who is an excellent hunter, to look around and mail me a pile of manuscript which is either in the hall closet or the bottom desk drawer.

There are many books about Cape Cod and it would seem strange to add one more. My first passionate desire to write about the Cape stemmed from my feeling that since I have lived in so many parts of the country I have had an overall experience of so many different areas that I might be able to sum up the special quality of this narrow land, not as a regional writer or a scientific observer but as a traveler coming home from far away.

"I had the strangest feeling when we crossed the bridge," said a midwestern friend. "I felt I was coming home."

I have given bits and pieces from the fabric measured in my own life, the place at the elbow of the Cape called Orleans. It cannot be complete, for there is always the unopened page of tomorrow, but the theme is unchanging—Cape Cod, my beautiful!